THE IONA
COMMUNITY

Personal Impressions
of the Early Years

THE IONA COMMUNITY

Personal Impressions of the Early Years

T. RALPH MORTON

THE SAINT ANDREW PRESS: EDINBURGH

First published in 1977 by
THE SAINT ANDREW PRESS
121 George Street, Edinburgh

© 1977   T. Ralph Morton

ISBN 0 7152 0357 6

To
GEORGE MACLEOD
in
Gratitude
Admiration
and
Affection

Printed and bound in Great Britain by
Scotprint Limited

Contents

CHAPTER ONE

What? How? Why?

The Iona Community has always aroused questions. What is it? How did it come into being? And why? It aroused questions at its beginning. It does so now, nearly forty years on. And in the years between men's questions never ceased. But they were not always the same questions.

Today those who know of it ask what its purpose is now. They wonder whether it has served its original purpose. Has it settled down to a comfortable and presumably useful old age? Or has it something new to say and to do? It has survived while some of its contemporaries and successors in experiment have either faded away or changed their shape beyond recognition. Has this survival been due to a strong conservative tradition among its members or to the presence of some revitalising spirit? With questionable omniscience some seem to be saying: 'We know all about what the Iona Community did in the past, but what is it doing now?'

These are some of the questions that men ask today. They are the questions that a veteran institution inspires. They are far from the questions that it aroused in its pioneering days. These were inspired by curiosity and expressed in hope or fear, suspicion or enthusiasm. The idea of a religious order in a Presbyterian church was novel. The plan of completing the restoration of a ruined mediaeval monastery was open to suspicion. And the views expressed seemed dangerously and oddly political. Was the proposed community a reactionary

1

movement, founded on a high-church tradition of worship, with its members playing at monks? Was it, indeed, tilted towards Rome? Or was it a deceptively dangerous movement, interested in pacifism and socialism, and committed to change? Was its direction really towards Moscow? Did it threaten the established order in Church and state. Or was it really a means of preserving things as they were?

These were the kind of questions men asked of the Iona Community more than thirty years ago. They were all about the future, even as the questions that men ask today are mainly about the past. This is inevitable, for in those days the Iona Community had no past, whereas today men doubt whether it has a future.

In the years between men asked other questions, practical questions. Who were the members of the Iona Community? What did they do? What was the relationship of the Iona Community to the Church? Was it a private society or part of the Church? Why was it composed only of men? Had it anything to offer to other people? Who made its decisions and directed its policy? Was it a group of 'yes-men'? And why did it make such an appeal to youth?

The story of the Iona Community could be regarded as the record of the questions men asked and the answers the Community tried to give. And, of course, these questions did not arise solely from curiosity about a strange, new little society. They were the reflection of the deeper questions that men were asking about the world and their own lives. The history of the Iona Community could illustrate the kinds of questions men were asking in the thirties, the forties, the fifties and the sixties of this century and the attempted answers of a small company of men.

But the story of the Iona Community could be read in quite a different way. It could be seen as illustrating the questions and problems that confront any enterprise in Church or society which is trying to break out into new ways of life and action. How far does such an enterprise depend on the vision and ability of one man? Are peculiar gifts of determination, endurance and even of authoritarianism necessary for success? How does such a man gather round him a continuing, developing group? How are they enabled to make their contribution? Outside interest and financial support are needed. How can these be assured without prejudicing the freedom of the experiment? Can any experiment achieve a lasting effect without some form of official recognition? What happens when the second generation takes over control? How does such a society hold the balance between the tradition of accepted and tried practice and the challenge of new ideas and a fresh vision?

Some day a proper history of the Iona Community will probably have to be written. In view of the present passion for histories of families, houses, businesses, transport and ideas, it is almost inconceivable that someone will not write a history of the Iona Community. This present record is no such history. Perhaps the time has not yet come for it. That history will demand the preparation of statistics, graphs of membership, the study of trends of interest. It will also demand a considerable measure of detachment. This present record certainly makes no claim to detachment. Whatever value it may have will lie in the fact that it is personal, subjective, prejudiced and individualistic.

But any enterprise that claims to be trying to explore new ways cannot be fully understood unless the subjective, individualistic prejudices of persons be taken into account. Its existence is generally due to a man of unique personality. Its continuance has depended on the contribution of a number of persons whose motives and expectations may be as varied as the gifts they bring. And generally for its success it has needed a co-operative response from a large number of people of all sorts who may be moved by very varying hopes and intentions. Even reaction against the enterprise will be inspired by

3

feelings as subjective and prejudiced. The air that any living experiment breathes is made up of hope and frustration, seeking and finding, insight and mutual service. Such personal experiences find little expression in minutes and none in statistics. But this personal quality is the life-blood of any creative enterprise. Certainly the Iona Community can never be understood in other terms.

So this present account is unashamedly the report of one man. His way of joining the Iona Community was peculiar and unlike any other member's. His service on the staff of the Community was longer than that of any one else, except the founder's. Every member of the Iona Community would have a different story to tell, for his reason for joining and the work he has done in the Community have been his own and unique. Each had discovered some truth about the world and about himself. The life of the Iona Community was enriched by — and was, indeed, made up of — the varied experiences, hopes and intentions of all its members. I, for one, would certainly claim that the experience of life in the Iona Community and experience of life in China were the two factors outside my family that brought joy and hope into life and made faith real. I give this personal account, not because I think my case important, but because the Iona Community can be understood only in these personal terms.

And as the account is so personal it seems right that I should begin by describing how I came to be in the Iona Community at all.

CHAPTER TWO

A Roundabout Road to Iona

China brought me into the Iona Community. Without the experience of life in China I cannot imagine how I ever would have gone back to Iona except as a visitor. But, on the other hand, I cannot now imagine life at all without that experience of China.

We came back from China in the summer of 1937 after I had spent twelve years there and my wife ten. These years had given to us uncountable gifts of understanding and of joy. Life in any foreign country must bring some understanding of life beyond what we take for granted in the familiar world of our home. Life in China brought the mysterious thrill of learning to see life through the eyes and minds of a people of a quite different but a very much older tradition than ours. To share their life was to see all life afresh. To think about the Christian Faith in their company was to see a new Jesus. Life in China brought us into the world of other people.

But these years had brought harsher gifts. In them we had known war and the enemy occupation of the country, for we were up in the North-East of China, known to foreigners but not to the Chinese as Manchuria. It was seized by Japanese troops in September 1931 and the land occupied to the great suffering of the people. This action marked the end of the frail hopes based on the League of Nations. Indeed the shots fired were the first shots of the Second World War, though we did not know it at the time. We witnessed the economic and political sufferings of an occupied people and their stoical endurance in the loss of hope. Persecution followed and came personally closer to us, for among those who suffered were the members of the Church, those with whom we lived and worked.

We had come to belong to a world of other people, of war, of occupation and of persecution and no one outside China seemed to know or to care about what was happening. The Western powers had closed their minds to the possibility of war. The Western churches had come to think that persecution had belonged to the middle ages and was gone. For our persecution began before the world realised what Hitler was doing to the Jews in Germany. This world of other people and of war and persecution had become our world, in which we had to interpret the Christian Faith and see the mission of the Church.

We came home to a country and a church in which we felt a bit lost. It was not that the world to which we returned seemed very different from the world we had left. It was rather that its people did not seem to see things as we saw them.

In September 1937 — two months after our return from China — a new play by J. B. Priestley was produced in London. It was called *I have been here before* and is one of his plays dealing with time. It tells of two sets of people staying by chance in a country inn in Yorkshire. They are joined by a stranger who somehow knows what they have been doing in the past and what will happen to them in the future. The present seems to take its meaning from time past and time to come. It is not that everything is explained and changed. It is rather that everything is changed and goes on as before. At the end of the play the stranger says to one of the people: 'You are now in the unusual and interesting position of a man who is moving out on a new time track, like a man who is suddenly born into a strange new world.'

'We have been here before' was the uncomfortable feeling

that grew upon us after we arrived home. There was the obvious joy of being once more at home, among familiar places and meeting old friends. There was the unexpected surprise of the varying greens and blues of hill and sea, so rich and changing compared with the faded, steady colours of North China. There was the relief of being no longer in a police state. But behind all this pleasant security we were increasingly aware of an uneasy feeling. The discomfort lay in an uncertain sense of time. We did not know whether we were living in the past or in the future. The present had ceased to have any meaning. The things that were happening in the Western world were things that had already happened to us. The future which seemed uncertain to others was known to us. This was uncomfortable enough. What made us wonder whether it was all a dream or a play about Yorkshire acted on a London stage was that no one else seemed to see what we saw or to react to current events as we did.

For us the world was a world to which war had already come. Their world seemed to us a dream world in which peace was still thought to prevail. Yet we were living in the same place, sharing the same point of time.

Soon after our return to Scotland I was called to St. Columba's Church in Cambridge and before the end of 1937 we were settled there. Cambridge might be thought to be as great a contrast to China as any place that could be found. But in many ways it was a good place to feel the pain of the world that was to be. It seemed almost Chinese in its sense of age and continuity and serenity. It differed in economic stability and therefore in an unconscious assumption of being above the problems of most other men. In its division between 'town' and 'gown' it revealed something of the Chinese scholar's superior attitude to other men. It was firmly rooted in the past but perhaps more than any other place it was aware of the future. Rutherford had split the atom in the Cavendish laboratory. He had just died and a table he had used was now

7

my study table — and still is. Physicists were working on the consequences of his work and were apprehensive.

But this was not what people in Cambridge were talking about in 1938. Three public events struck Cambridge more closely and were the pointers to the more immediate future.

First there was the Spanish Civil War. This was very much at the top of men's minds and at the front of their conversation. For Cambridge was involved. Many of her sons were fighting for liberty in Spain. Some had been killed. The horror and cruelty of that war were not just items of news in the papers. Cambridge was committed to one side as Hitler was committed to the other. The victory of Franco was a sad omen for the future.

Then there was the reception of Jewish refugees from Austria and Germany. Many distinguished scholars had already come with their families. They were welcomed by the colleges. We had some in our congregation. Then children began to arrive. This sponsoring and caring for Jewish children was an activity in which the Cambridge churches were deeply involved, not least St. Columba's. So Cambridge learned something also about persecution, even if, fortunately, only at second-hand through the refugees it welcomed.

The third event was Hitler's occupation of Czechoslovakia. For most people in Cambridge this was a less personal, more distant event. But for some it wasn't. Many Czech theological students had studied in Cambridge and most of them worshipped in St. Columba's. Close links were maintained with them. When Neville Chamberlain at Munich gave in to Hitler, for many a sense of betrayal was greater than any feeling of relief.

I was coming back from Oxford through London when the news of Munich broke. Reserves had already been called up. I had gone to Oxford thinking that we might be at war before I got home. In the train to London, in the streets of London and in the train to Cambridge men talked in an unusually open way. They seemed reluctantly relieved that war was averted. But uppermost in their minds was shame: that we had bought peace for ourselves by the betrayal of another country. I was surprised that the general feeling was so strong. There was also apparent among the younger men a feeling of regret: not that they had wanted to fight but that if war had come they would have known what to do and now they didn't.

To us, back from the tensions of occupation and persecution, their attitude seemed more intelligible than that of some of the leading pacifists at home. These welcomed peace at any price, hoped for the final collapse of the League of Nations and seemed to have little thought for the sufferings of people. Their acquiescence in what was happening seemed to us quite terrifying. One evening we met George Lansbury, the leader of the Labour Party and leader of the Opposition of that time. He expressed his relief at Munich and told us what a kind man Hitler was. He had just had an interview with him. Hitler had been told that he had a bad foot and had prepared a stool for him to rest it on. Then he said: 'What did Czechoslovakia matter anyway? It was a new artificial state.' When we muttered 'Bohemia' he did not seem to know what we were talking about.

'We have been here before.' All that was happening — the Spanish Civil War, the persecution of the Jews, the betrayal of Czechoslovakia — reminded us of what we had witnessed in China. What had happened there was being repeated in the West. But others did not seem to read the signs. We did not feel that we quite belonged to this brave old world. We felt that we were acting a part in someone else's play. This feeling of artificiality was made all the worse by the settled, impregnable, high-minded life of Cambridge.

To live in Cambridge before the War was otherwise an exceedingly pleasant and a very interesting experience. The old social conventions of calling and entertaining still held and Bloomsbury still cast its lingering aesthetic shade. The friendliness, charm and unreality of Cambridge were summed up in a visit that C. D. Dodd made soon after we arrived. He came to suggest that he put forward my name for the vacant chair of Chinese. I protested my incompetence and suggested that they appoint a Chinese. He thought this an excellent suggestion but came back later to say that those responsible thought that it was necessary that the professor should speak English. They appointed a Czech.

But it was comfortable and encouraging to find in Cambridge and in St. Columba's in particular so many people concerned about the world, generous in help and aware that new patterns of social life had to be found. But as one moved out into wider groupings one found a depressing detachment, especially among church people. In our first years I was asked to do a great deal of speaking about China. The constant response to any mention of persecution was: 'Well, I suppose a little persecution would do us good.' It was invariable and infuriating. It revealed a complete ignorance of the nature of persecution and its cost. It was thought of as a mild stimulant which would awaken a keener sense of duty. It was really a rather superior attitude. It implied that we in this country would never let ourselves get into such a position, but that we could show a little sympathy to those who were foolish and weak. They did not recognise that they had any responsibility for allowing them to be in this situation.

It was in fact not easy to adjust to the attitude of the Church at home after twelve years in the Church in China. The difference of attitude might not have been so striking if we had come back to the old, peaceful, settled life of Britain. But events showed that we were in the same world as we had known in China, even if not in the same kind of Church.

The Church overseas based its work on three principles, at least so far as its missionaries were concerned. The first was the necessity of learning the language of the people, not only as the only means of making contact with people but also as the essential way of coming to an understanding of their ways of life and thought. And this was a task that was never finished. The second was the work of helping to build up a pattern of corporate Christian living which was not confined to what went on in church buildings but had to do with the home and neighbours and work. And, thirdly, the missionary Church had always found political involvement inevitable. From the beginning of its enterprise education and medicine had been seen as naturally and inescapably part of the Gospel. We have only to think of the heat generated by education and medicine in Britain and in the United States to realise how fundamentally political these topics are. Wherever the Church has carried the Gospel into a non-Christian society it has worked on these three principles — of language, community and politics.

The Church at home did not seem to recognise these principles at all. It worked on other priorities. It seemed to think that all it had to do was to recall people to religion and to preach morality. It was not that the Church at home was not interested in language. It was very interested in its own language and in the language of its past. The theological fashion of the time lay in the revival of old orthodoxies, in going back to what Aquinas or Luther or Calvin had said. It was not interested in the language that people outside were using. It was as if it were saying to those outside and to its own young people: 'If you want to understand the Christian Faith you must learn our archaic language.' To a returned missionary this sounded not only strange but blasphemous.

One of the reasons why the Church seemed so content to use a secret, archaic language of its own was that it was not really concerned with the life that its members were living in the world. It was, therefore, not speaking intelligibly even to them. The life of the Church was limited to activities that went

11

on in church buildings and sometimes in the houses of members. But such activities were mainly confined to the promotion of ecclesiastical interests and the discussion of private duty.

But perhaps it was the home Church's detachment from political concerns that struck a returned missionary most sharply. The issues he had faced in China no doubt strengthened the contrast. The Church there had indeed failed because it had not been sufficiently awake to political issues but it had been forced to heed them and to be involved.

It was into this situation that George MacLeod, speaking a language we could understand, came to give us hope.

He did not come at our invitation or because we were there, though we had known each other since we had been students. His visit had been arranged before we came to Cambridge. He had been invited to preach at the annual conference of the Laymen's Association of the Presbyterian Church of England. But he was our first visitor in Cambridge. On the morning after his arrival the post brought the duplicated statements of his plan to found the Iona Community. These typed sheets were the first we were to see of that endless scatter of reports, documents, proposals which marks his race down the years. So it chanced that we were the first people, outside those immediately implicated, who saw the plan and heard him expound it. He insisted on our going to Iona in the summer to witness the start of the Community. And every year, so long as we were in Cambridge, he came to meet students, to talk with groups about the meaning of the Faith and the mission of the Church, to lead conferences and to preach. We cannot look back on those six years in Cambridge without seeing him as a very vital part of them.

We would have been very glad to welcome him in any case for the inspiration he brought to so many young people in Cambridge. But we were peculiarly encouraged because he, from an entirely different background of experience, seemed to see the mission and the difficulties of the Church in the same way as we did from our experience in China.

He recognised the problem of language. From his years in Govan he knew that the Church was not speaking in words that ordinary men could understand. He knew that it was not a matter of simplifying the vocabulary but of speaking in terms of the worries and the joys, the fears and the hopes, the wonder and the despair of men in the world today. The Church had to take communism and science seriously if only to understand what influenced men's thinking.

Then he saw that the great need of the Church was to find community again. It was for this that he resigned his charge of Govan and was setting out to found a new little community on Iona. But his concern was not this little embryonic community so much as the common life of the Church. He knew that the Church had to become less respectable and more open if it was to fulfil its mission. He knew that it must recover a more truly corporate life of its own, expressed in action and supported by prayer and worship. He did not see this as an abstract theory but as something to be lived out with people in particular places and in particular situations.

And then he knew that no one could talk the language of men today and no one could be serious about corporate life without raising political questions. And he spoke as one who had already acted politically. He had taken action to help the unemployed in Govan in the years of the Depression. In the year previous to his coming to Cambridge he had fought and won Dick Shepherd's campaign as a pacifist in the rectorial election in the University of Glasgow. He had offended many by his espousal of unpopular causes. But he knew that the Church has nothing to say to men if it eschewed politics.

He made the mission of the Church mean something again for many, because he made it broad-based and demanding and, above all, because he acted before he spoke.

This may seem a very long and far too personal introduction

to the Iona Community. But we cannot appreciate the mood out of which the Iona Community arose unless we somehow have the feel of that apprehensive period before the outbreak of the Second World War. We cannot justly judge of George MacLeod's purpose unless we understand how aware he was of the fact of a changing world, of the likelihood of war and of its appalling consequences for Church and nation. The immediate cause of the founding of the Iona Community was the tragedy of the economic depression of the thirties and the Church's failure to do anything about it. But his thinking was never merely local or narrowly national. And war when it came only underlined these universal factors.

CHAPTER THREE

Its Only Begetter

The Iona Community came into existence at a particular time and at a particular place. Its purpose and the form it took cannot be understood without some imaginative appreciation of that time and place and of the man to whom solely it owed its existence.

The place was Govan, on the Clyde and now inside the city of Glasgow, and the time the end of the thirties, that tragic decade of economic depression. And the man was George MacLeod, minister of the Old Parish of Govan during these years.

The Church had been in Govan for nearly fourteen hundred years. But Govan had changed. It had changed from being a country village to become an overcrowded part of the city of Glasgow: from being a place where men farmed and fished to a place where they built ships. But in the depression that struck Britain and America in the thirties shipbuilding had ceased. The yards were empty. The men were idle. In Govan there was no other employment. It was estimated that 80 per cent of the men of Govan were unemployed and saw no hope of employment. All that they could do was to stand at the street corners and talk and draw their inadequate 'dole' and watch their children suffer. The Church from its centuries-old position preached and served. And, under George MacLeod, it did both with power and imagination. Forthright preaching, often broadcast on the radio, new experiments in worship, the use of music, art and drama, congregational participation and all the rest of the things we talk about now: all these were there. The services were crowded with people from all over Glasgow but not with the unemployed men of Govan.

Less dramatic but more demanding was the social work initiated on behalf of the men of Govan and their families. This was before the days of the Welfare State. Work was found to keep some occupied. Clubs were opened for them. And for all this men and money had to be found. This work pointed the way to new civic and national action. It was work that had to be done for its own sake. It was probably hoped that it would reconcile men to the Church. But social service did not bring the men of Govan into church any more than worship did. Men did not feel that the Church belonged to their world. It was not that they rejected the faith of the Church or that they felt that they could make no claim on the Church. It was rather that they were angry with the Church: they felt that it had betrayed them and its faith. The Church was not interested in industry and therefore it was not interested in them. The Church was interested in what went on in the home, not in what went on in the yard: in how men spent their money, not in how they made it or failed to. To George MacLeod this was a judgment on the Church and a call to it to recover its essential mission. The Church had first to realise that these men belonged to the Church and then to learn their language and how together they could serve the world.

One episode gave hope in those depressing years. Fingleton Mill, a disused and partly ruined mill on the southern outskirts of Glasgow, was taken over as a holiday centre for the children and youth of Govan. The repair work was carried out by a team of unemployed men and a few young ministers and students. This proved to be something quite different from welfare work. The men were on a real job, using their own

16

skills, on a job that was worth doing because it was for others and in which they were the craftsmen and the ministers and students were the unskilled labourers. The success of this little enterprise suggested bigger things. Was this a way by which the gap between Church and industry might be bridged?

This experience of the effect of industrial men and ministers working together was fused in George MacLeod's mind with the dream that he and others had had of the ruined Abbey on Iona restored for modern use. Out of this union the Iona Community was born.

George MacLeod resigned his charge of the parish of Govan and set off to start his little community on Iona.

His action was inevitably misunderstood. Some said that he was on the road to Rome. Wasn't he going to restore a monastery? And wasn't Govan very 'high church'? Others feared that he was heading for Moscow. He advocated pacifism and discussed politics. Some said that he was just being romantic. Others again said that what he was doing was wrong and contrary to the law of the Church of Scotland. In the second issue of *The Coracle*, the little magazine that he started in October 1938, he protested: 'It is not a return to Rome. . . . It is not a pacifist community. . . . It is not a visionary movement . . . seeking helplessly to play at being Franciscans. . . . It is on the contrary an exceedingly calculated movement within the normal purpose of the Church.'[1]

No surveys or computers had been used to help him in his calculations, but he was right in insisting that his scheme was devised to meet particular and immediate needs. That it was practicable and related to the administration of the Church was demonstrated by events. The original paper outlining the scheme showed this clearly. It could be called the founding document of the Iona Community, though the name of Iona or the word 'community' never appears in it. It begins by listing the three needs of the Church of Scotland, seen in 1938

1. *The Coracle*, No. 2, May 1939, p. 18.

by George MacLeod as adequate staffing, experiment in the technique of fellowship and the preservation of its presbyterian witness. These rather pedestrian needs were expounded in more vivid words. Then followed what was called the Practical Application:

> 'That a brotherhood be formed immediately, composed of licentiates recently out of the Divinity Halls and also fully qualified artisans, who would pledge their services to the Brotherhood for a limited period. All would receive the same pay during their period in the Fellowship — all found and fifty pounds a year. While artisans would come for such periods as their labour was required, licentiates would normally undertake to serve for two years.[2]

The manual work of the brotherhood would be the completion of the rebuilding of the Abbey on Iona. The ruins of the Abbey, the Nunnery and the graveyard, the Relig Odhran, had been given by the eighth Duke of Argyll to the Church of Scotland and vested in a Trust whose title deed expressed the hope that the ruins would be restored and when restored would be open to the worship of all churches. By public subscription and by contract labour the Abbey church had been restored before the First World War and was used for worship in summer. But there the restoration had stopped. The restoration of the Abbey church or cathedral and the dream of what whole restoration might still be led to the institution by Sir David Russell, after the War, of retreats on Iona for theological students to give to the future ministers of the Church a new idea of devotional discipline and a new sense of mission. The partial restoration of the Benedictine buildings and the success of the retreats suggested the idea of a community and indeed indicated the basic form that it was to take.

But the plan as George MacLeod saw it was to develop along two new significant lines. The work would not be put out

2. This document is reprinted in *The Coracle*, No. 36, March 1960, p. 6.

to contract but be carried out by the members themselves, craftsmen and ministers working together. For the object was not just to complete the rebuilding as quickly as possible but for a group of men to learn some new lessons by living and working and worshipping together, and work would only be done in the summer months. For the greater part of the year men would be back at their ordinary industrial or ecclesiastical jobs. George MacLeod claimed, rightly as it proved, that men in industry would welcome the chance of expressing themselves through their craft without subjection to the profit of their bosses. He also claimed, perhaps with more doubtful accuracy, that the ministers would find living and working with the craftsmen an 'essentially exhilarating experience'.

And, secondly, the work of rebuilding would be on those parts of the building given over to ordinary daily life: the refectory, the dormitories, the library, the wash-houses, the kitchen and all the other domestic offices. These were the buildings that men would occupy and use when they began to live there. The questions that would arise would not be about worship and daily services and the discipline of prayer but about all the tensions of a mixed company of people living together.

This was a revolutionary plan to put before the Church of Scotland. It could, indeed, have been paralleled by many other schemes on paper, now preserved in reports to committees or in magazine articles. It was not the plan itself that was so remarkable as that it was so quickly carried out. Within a few weeks of its publication it was in operation. It looked like a crazy dream but it was prepared and carried out with military precision and efficiency. Approval had been given by the trustees of the Abbey. Leaders in Church and society in Scotland had agreed to be sponsors. Everything was ready except men and money when the scheme was made public in the spring of 1938.

The document gives little hint of this. It might have been read as a quite impracticable scheme. It might well have ended up in a waste-paper basket. It was indeed written in a very low-key style. But, then, it was intended for the trustees of ecclesiastical property, the heads of theological colleges and the conveners of church committees. But all who received it knew George MacLeod. He was the originator of the plan and the sole reason why anything got started. Our understanding of the experiment cannot be based only on the study of paper. It has to include some knowledge of the man himself and some understanding of his impact on other people.

Careful planning and the intention to implement what he planned lay behind the document. They explain why the plan got going. They also indicate the force of the impact he made on other people and particularly on those who were young. He was not discussing theories but promising action. His scheme was a plan of campaign, not the diagnosis of a situation. Of course there was plenty of diagnosis in what he wrote. It could be wild but it was all the more exciting for that. What shone through was the detail and the realism of the plan. He gave people the idea that there was something they could do. He gave them hope. Of course he offended some and shocked others. Some accused him of being rash and impetuous and disregardful of the ways of working of the Church. Others excused him for the sake of what he was doing. The sight of someone in the Church who intended to do something and would obviously bring his intention to fruition was a wonderful sign of hope to many.

And first of all the plan involved himself. He was not waiting to see how others would react. He was not waiting for someone else to act first. He committed himself before he asked others to commit themselves. And he committed himself far more deeply. His resignation of the parish of Govan was proof of this.

But these qualities, though attractive and rare, might have

20

been harnessed to a dull scheme that could even have put others off.

His real power lay elsewhere.

When he put his novel scheme before the men he wanted, his power to excite and draw them lay in his common touch. For all his poetic language and radical ideas he began with men where they were. His proposition may have sounded very strange to them and his way of putting it often incomprehensible. But they knew basically what he was talking about. They and he shared the same basic belief — and prejudices. His innate conservatism is strong. It lies in his unquestioning acceptance of inherited moral and religious beliefs. In ethics he recognises absolute standards which for him are beyond discussion. What he will discuss is our application of them. What he will question is our treatment of those who infringe them. The key to his social concern and to many of his activities is to be found in his life-long interest in juvenile delinquents. This began long before the Iona Community was thought of. He may retire from other activities. He never retires from this. In theology he does not question the beliefs of the Church nor even the traditional ways of expressing them. But he could take what was dogmatic or controversial and make it relevant and exciting and, therefore, intelligible for the moment. His reading of the Bible is simple. He assumes that the Bible means what it seems to say. He can appreciate the questions that pacifism and healing raise but he sees the Biblical teaching as clear. In the same way he is never a rebel in the Church. He is not even a reformer. His loyalty is too strong to permit criticism except of the Church's failure to live out its accepted faith. His desire is to revive its tarnished brightness: to make strong what was weak and to make compassionate what was peevish.

This may seem an out-dated attitude forty years later. It does not make an instant appeal to youth today. But there is no doubt that this blend of a simple but imaginatively expressed acceptance of beliefs and attitudes with a passionate intention to see them manifest in new and positive action made many in the thirties listen to him and follow him.

Without this common touch he could have made no wide appeal. What he said and did was something men could understand. They did not always agree. Pacifism and his own brand of socialism did not always convert his followers. But they showed that he was serious. He was doing something and doing something new. He gave men something to argue about, something to oppose, something to follow.

This common touch by itself would have made him a man whom people respected, consulted, used. Something more was needed to make his scheme come alive. George MacLeod's appeal had another quality that fused together his innate conservatism and his radical opinions and gave them life. Some would say that he is essentially romantic. Others would say that he thinks and speaks in pictures. Certainly he speaks in pictures. This is probably because he thinks in pictures but more because he knows that this is how most men think. And pictures involve selection and an almost inevitable exaggeration and even distortion. In this sense there is no doubt that George MacLeod is a romantic, as are most people at heart. But he is a romantic who is not satisfied merely to paint his pictures in words. They are of no value to him unless they are expressed in flesh and blood, in wood and stone.

To call his community after Iona was romantic and he knew it. It appealed to his sense of history. It spoke to his sense of wonder and of beauty. It represented continuity and renewal. But it was a romantic dream that could be made into something practical, modern and painful. He knew that most men were not interested in diagnosis and theory. It was this ability to put practical demands in attractive pictures that moved men. Without the romance there would have been no movement. Without the physical demands of a material job there would have been no response.

This fusion of vision and commitment, manifest on Iona, was felt by many especially in his conduct of worship. Today, when so many of the sons of those to whom George MacLeod appealed in the thirties are puzzled and even irritated by the worship of the Church, it may be difficult to recall the days when men knew that they wanted to worship but did not know how to do it. He made worship a happy activity to many by helping them to see the wonder of God's world and to know that they were committed to possible actions. His preaching startled, intrigued and interested people but it was his leading of worship, in the intimacy of the Abbey, that led them to understanding and action. Preaching is cerebral. Worship involves the imagination and the will. We can never understand the beginning of the Iona Community or, indeed, understand George MacLeod himself unless we realise that this was at bottom the appeal he made to men. And this was what drew men to Iona and still affects them when they get there. George MacLeod's greatest gift was to be able to make people see a vision and to know what it meant to be committed to it.

This explains why Iona appealed to so many people of so many different types. It appealed to the conservative and to the radical, to the ritualist and to those who wished to be free of all forms, to the social worker and to the Borstal boy.

Of course, many were suspicious. Some were offended. And some were just envious. It would not be much of a new experiment if some people did not misunderstand and others oppose. The determination to get something done attracted some and offended others. There are always those who consider it more important that everything should be done correctly than that something should be done at all. Then there are those — and, in Scotland, many — who feel that it is unfair that someone should do what they themselves cannot or will not do. There are always those who will ask: 'Who does he think he is?' These objections are not made of those who make speeches or write books. For anyone can make a speech or write a book and there is no necessity on others to listen or to read. And you can listen or read with interest, curiosity, opposition or amusement and not be the least affected in your actions. But action itself is different. What one man does, no one else can do, except in imitation. And action always involves other people. And, therefore, action affects events. And when an action is intended to affect the situation in which men live, when it is 'an exceedingly calculated movement within the normal purpose of the Church' then some people are bound to be suspicious and resentful.

The scheme as propounded in 1938 seemed in its practical, low-key way to suggest that the sponsors, if they thought there was anything in it, might want to advertise for someone to inaugurate and run it. But a significant paragraph at the end said:

> 'For the purpose of its inception, I would myself be prepared to leave my present work at any time now and would undertake to stand by the Experiment full time, resisting any conceivable inducements, for a term of five years. For such time during that period as I remained unmarried I would offer my services without reward.'

Not that there was ever any question in the minds of the sponsors or of George MacLeod himself as to who must be the leader. No experiment of such a nature can begin and continue without a man of exceptional vision, intention, determination and attraction who sees the work as in some peculiar way his own.

There could have been no Iona Community without George MacLeod. And the Iona Community cannot be understood in all its peculiar achievements, difficulties and failures unless we have some kind of picture of George MacLeod as a man.

As with many creative people it is easier to understand the nature of his unique creativeness if we know something of his ancestry and of his early life.

His ancestry set the pattern of his life. And we do not have to go farther back than his great-grandfather to find that pattern. John Prebble, in his book on the Highland clearances, writes of the latter as one of the Highland ministers who spoke up for the people. He gives this description of him:

'Speakers from the Highlands were welcomed to London, and one of the most popular was the handsome, white-haired Moderator of the Church of Scotland, Norman MacLeod. He was a Highlander with a rich and musical voice that charmed more guineas from the purses and reticules of his audience than the sense of what he said. He was one of the few ministers of his Church who was beloved in the Highlands. He liked to roam Morven in a kilt of his tartan, talk in the Gaelic of old days and old ways, but at the London Mansion House in March 1836 he was dressed in the black of his cloth.'

George MacLeod's grandfather, also Norman MacLeod and also a Moderator, was a popular preacher, a friend of Queen Victoria, who worked to improve the condition of the inhabitants of the slums of Glasgow, who wrote hymns, edited a paper and rejected a novel by Anthony Trollope because of impropriety –– it describes young people dancing. His father, Sir John MacLeod, Bt., was a Tory Member of Parliament for two Glasgow constituencies in succession.

To balance this clerical, 'establishment' background, with its strong strain of romantic action, he is on the mother's side of a Quaker, radical, English tradition. His other great-grandfather John Fielden, radical M.P. for Oldham, was known as 'Honest John Fielden' and had charge in Parliament of the 'Ten Hours Bill' from 1840 to 1847 when it became law. These were two very different traditions. But they were united in public service, social responsibility and willingness to take the unpopular side.

George MacLeod's education agreed with his background:

3. John Prebble, *The Highland Clearances* (Penguin, 1963), p. 164.

Winchester, Oxford, Edinburgh and New York. As might be expected of a man of poetry and picture rather than of text-book, his time in the army during the First World War was more formative than his years of formal education. As an adjutant in the Argyll and Sutherland Highlanders he developed his administrative ability. Years later his colleagues felt that he enjoyed nothing more fully than the minute and efficient organisation of occasions such as the visit of the Queen to Iona and the Fourteenth Centenary of the landing of Columba on Iona. At the same time in the trenches he gained an understanding of and admiration for men with whom his education had not brought him into contact — the men from the yards and slums of Govan. To admiration for their endurance and humour was added a compassion which was always to place him on the side of the under-privileged. It was this that made him a socialist and yet brought no conscious break with the tradition of his far from socialist ancestors.

This sympathy brought him from a church in the west end of Edinburgh to Govan in 1930. He came not as a man with a mission to the unfortunate but as one coming to where he now knew he belonged. He did not choose to live in the manse in a nearby residential area but in a flat in the community centre next to the church in the centre of Govan. Here he decided that the Church must do something quite radical in the way of experiment if it was to find its life and mission for and with industrial men. That the Church must act meant that he must do something himself.

His double action of resigning his successful charge of Govan and setting off for Iona in a little coasting steamer, with a dozen young men and the prefabricated sections of the hut in which they were to live, illustrated in a vivid way many of his peculiar qualities: willingness to take risks and to abandon an obviously successful career; curiosity as to new ideas and a desire to find new ways; a passion for symbolic and imaginative action; a determination to act on his own and not to wait for someone else's lead. Those who envied his successful career suspected him of hidden ambitions. The Church of Scotland Moderator of the year asked my wife: 'What does George want? He's had St. Cuthbert's and Govan. What more does he want?' But his action helped younger men to realise that they need not follow the set course; that there were other things to do. Some accused him of having a restless mind. Some annual visitors to Iona would ask: 'What is the line this year?' Anthroposophy? Money? The idea of a United Church of Great Britain? Pacifism? But this width of interest opened men's minds to what was happening in the world and to new possibilities. It taught them to think adventurously. And all the time, and through it all, his wit sparkled and he told stories and men laughed. It would be wrong to overlook the power of laughter. It pointed, as humour always does, to something deeper than appearances and a truth that words can never adequately express.

George MacLeod offered his services free to get the experiment started. He said that he would do so as long as he was unmarried. It should be said that when, later, he married, he continued to give his services free. It is obvious that it would have been difficult for someone not a bachelor with private means to have done what he did. And what he did demanded more courage and faith than these words super-ficially indicate. The trustees of the Abbey might be said to be rash in agreeing to a scheme for the completion of the rebuilding of the ruins when there were as yet no funds provided for the purpose. But they were not so irresponsible as to agree without some guarantee. George MacLeod personally guaranteed that he, or his heirs, would be financially responsible for the completion of the work. This was an act of faith that involved considerable risk. The final cost of the rebuilding was well over £100,000 and if, on account of the collapse of the Iona Community, the work had

27

had to be finished by commercial contract it would have cost very much more. Fortunately George MacLeod had inherited the ability to get money out of people. The raising of money was always his responsibility, so long as he remained leader.

Would anything have started without the imaginative compassion that the years of depression in Govan aroused? Would anything have started without his ambitious commitment? Would anything have started if George MacLeod had not enjoyed a privileged position? Would anything have got going without the romance of rebuilding on Iona? Would anything have started without George MacLeod, for all these made up the man?

This is not a merely rhetorical question. The Church talks a lot about the need for experiments in mission and for the necessity of finding new ways of life. But how far does any form of renewal depend on the emergence of a creative person? It is difficult to think of any significant new movement in the past that has not depended on such a person. Success of such an experiment seems to depend on a leader with vision, with a commitment that does not think in terms of a short-time appointment and with a certain ruthlessness.

But when we consider such experiments in the Church and particularly when we think of the vital importance of their originators, two points have to be made.

The first is that you can never treat the emergence of a leader as an entirely isolated event. It is easy to see him as a solitary rebel protesting against the current trend. He is as often responding to fears and hopes and urges felt by many others. He acts on his own but soon he finds that there are others, often in surprising places, who are thinking the same thoughts and even doing the same kind of things. The success of any experiment depends a great deal on this striking of the hour. This was certainly true of George MacLeod's action in founding the Iona Community. The Iona Community had from the beginning its kindred movements from which it drew

28

inspiration and strength. There was Sigtuna in Sweden. There were movements in the Netherlands. Things were happening in Asia and Africa. And after the war there were others: Agapé in Italy, Taizé in France, the Evangelical Academies in Germany, Kerk en Wereld in Holland. Most of these had their powerful founders who had a like vision and who also impressed their peculiar stamp on their creations.

The second point is a double question. How does the Church use the creative people who emerge? And how do the experiments they start get on to the next stage? And how does the Church accept them? Does the Church by opposition or neglect make its creative sons rebels and brand them as heretics? Or does the Church by kindly patronage take the sting out of their actions and degrade them to a footnote in its history? How does a movement started by a powerful leader get on to the next stage without losing its impetus and vision? How does it make its significant contribution to the on-going life of Church and society?

This is not a problem for the Church alone. Politics and industry know it also. There have been cases of new businesses, founded and set triumphantly going by a man of vision and drive, which have run into difficulties when he gave up control. New political parties have foundered when the founder retired.

But it is a peculiarly urgent problem for the Church when it is faced with new tasks in a new world and has to find new ways of life and witness. It will be in dangerous case if it cannot take into its changing life the vision of the prophet and the results of new experiments.

But it is perhaps wrong to talk of George MacLeod as a prophet, as if his desire was to be a voice crying in the wilderness. His aim was to found a brotherhood. His passionate desire was to find a way to renew the corporate life of the Church. He knew from his time in Govan how tragically the Church was failing in its corporate life, and therefore in its life

29

with men in the world. The experiment on which he embarked was an experiment in life together. He was the Community before there were any other members. It was his doing. And it was something new. Its creation was his unique achievement.

CHAPTER FOUR

The Birth and Growth of a Community

George MacLeod was the founder and only begetter of the Iona Community. It was his inspired achievement. And it was deliberate. It might have been more in keeping with the mood of the time and with the usual practice of churchmen if he had written a book to expound an idea or set up a new society to reform the Church. But he did not see these as things that the Church lacked. What it did lack was community — the sense of belonging to each other and to all other men. He had known real, if limited, community in the army. He knew that there was community among the unemployed men of Govan. But these experiences of community seemed only to emphasise the lack of it in the Church.

He knew what was needed in its simplicity. He knew that men had to learn to live together. He knew that it was only as men learned to live together that they would learn to understand the Christian Faith. His unique creative action was to call into being a little company of men to live, work and worship together. He knew what he was trying to do. Did he foresee the outcome? He did not claim to. In the first issue of *The Coracle* he wrote, regarding men's craving at that time for community: 'Where in this bubbling world of Collective Experiment, then, does the Iona Community seek to take its place? It is to be no more than a laboratory of co-operative living in which we hope to discover a little more of what the place of the Church is in this particular commotion. . . . It is a

Laboratory working under the sign of all good laboratories — which is a Question Mark.'[1]

The first thing to be done — indeed the only thing necessary — was to find men prepared to join. Those who would join would be taking a leap in the dark. George MacLeod knew, from his experience in Govan, what needed to be done and what he wanted to do and how he meant to do it. Those who joined could have only a vague idea of what was involved for them. There would have been no Iona Community but for George MacLeod. But there could be no community till they joined. Its future would depend on the kind of men they were and the kind of life they created for themselves.

There are many ways of forming a brotherhood. They depend on the choice of the recruiting field and on the method of selection of candidates. How were the first members of the Iona Community chosen? Where did they come from? And why did they come? All that was decided was that half of them would be ministers and the other half would be craftsmen. And all would be young.

The ministers came from among those who as students had worked with him in Govan or had been on retreat on Iona or had heard him speak and were interested in his plan. They came from the theological faculties of the four old Scottish universities. The craftsmen were recruited by more fortuitous contacts. One would come because he knew George MacLeod. One came because he arrived on Iona on a walking tour and became interested. Another had heard George MacLeod speak at a meeting.

Of the original company who gathered on Iona in June 1938, George MacLeod wrote:

'It is one thing to shoot an article at an unoffending public in the beginning of May with the news that we intended building log huts round the Abbey and starting there a Community of Clergy and artisans. It is quite another thing

1. *The Coracle*, No. 1, October 1938, p. 3.

within six weeks to have the whole thing in motion . . . yet so it happened. . . . By the middle of June a team was in shape. Four ministers who had already been at work in parishes; four Divinity students, one from each Divinity hall; an architect, a doctor, a secretary and seven artisans had volunteered their services. Indeed it is right to point out that many others wrote offering to come. . . . In the end we took only those who were personally known to us and on whom we might reckon to be of specific service in the actual labour or in the plotting of our future purposes. . . . It was a slightly dazed company — truth to tell — who sat down for their first meal together in the open, beneath the old Abbey and beside the solitary log cabin that was to be their dormitory, sitting- and dining-room for the next three months. Few knew more than two of the others previously. The majority were sitting in a company of complete strangers.'

Why had they come?

The ministers would have answered that they had joined the Iona Community because they realised the difficulty of the job that awaited them when they went to a parish and their inadequacy to deal with it. They did not question, as some of their successors would today, the modern feasibility of the idea of the parish. They accepted it as the obvious way of the Church's working. But they felt that in college they had not been prepared for it. They knew that it was not a task that could any longer be undertaken by one man working on his own. The solitary parish minister attending to his flock might have suited rural Scotland in the eighteenth century. It was impossible in industrial Scotland in the twentieth. They were attracted by the idea of beginning their full-time work in a team, engaged with working men in manual work and then, after their summer on Iona, working in a small team of ministers in an industrial parish.

Their recognition that only a team ministry would help them reflected their sense of isolation in Church and society. They were looking for some new way of life, some attractive and compelling discipline, which they knew had to be corporate and not individual. The project of finishing the rebuilding of the Abbey, far from appealing to them as a romantic escape, promised them working contact with ordinary men and, through George MacLeod, confrontation with some of the urgent political issues of the day, particularly unemployment and the threat of war.

The craftsmen volunteered from simpler motives. What attracted them was the chance of a job at a time of acute unemployment, the opportunity of exercising their craft in a job not ruled by the necessity of someone else's profit and curiosity about the strange way of life offered to them. They would not have claimed any particular religious motivation. Indeed they were rather scared by the religious pattern of the life into which they were entering. But their reasons were probably as altruistic as the ministers'.

The composition and the life of the group were determined by George MacLeod. This was inevitable. The group had come into existence because of his realisation of the needs of Govan in particular and of industrial Scotland as a whole and of his conviction of the need of change in the life and witness of the Church if it were to meet these needs. A different idea would have recruited a different set of men. If the experiment had been simply in community living a more varied and an easier group might well have been found. But the group was not chosen for its own good or for the interest of its members. It was chosen for a specific task: the discovery of a new way of life for the Church in industrial Scotland in the middle of the twentieth century. Ministers and craftsmen were wanted because in this task they were the problem classes for the Church: the craftsmen because they were rarely seen in church and the ministers because they were apt to be seen only in church and were indeed often regarded as the Church. And the work of rebuilding on Iona was chosen, not merely because of its historic importance and its symbolism —

though these were never absent from George MacLeod's thinking — but because it offered work in which the craftsmen would be the teachers and the ministers the apprentices.

The plan was that the work should be done only in the summer months. In September all returned to the mainland: the ministers to work in pairs in selected parishes, the craftsmen to find what work they could in the labour market. The aim was not to take men out of their situation or to offer them a different and secure setting for their lives. It was a business rather of their coming to see the situation they were in and of working out together a creative way of living in it. The time on Iona was not intended as a retreat but as a chance of living with others at very close quarters on a common job of manual work and of learning how work and worship were related. It was an experience for which neither the ministers nor the craftsmen were in any way prepared, for George MacLeod was the only one of the group old enough to have served in the First World War.

It was not an easy life. A small island offers little in the way of escape or distraction. In those early days it lacked the amenities that electricity brought in the late fifties. It was rather like living on board a ship. The weather was often bad. The work could be monotonous and irksome. Privacy was impossible. Worship — morning and evening — was part of the pattern of the day. In the early years it was always conducted by George MacLeod himself. Worship, indeed, gave contact with others on the island. For it was always public worship. It was through the daily worship that many who were interested or curious were brought into living contact with the Community.

For all Iona's isolation, it was life lived in the public eye. The Community could not escape publicity nor its members escape into anonymity. They were conspicuous through the uniform that they wore at evening worship and on Sunday mornings. The uniform was the navy-blue suit of the sailor and fisherman, the accepted dress of the men of the islands; but with navy-blue shirt and tie. 'Who are these sinister men in dark clothes?' Princess Margaret asked when she attended worship in the Abbey with the Queen. The uniform was common to ministers and craftsmen and indicated the nature of their common work. It differentiated them from other people, whereas at the morning service when they wore their working clothes they were identified with the working population.

When the work of rebuilding was finished, men ceased to wear working clothes and ceased too to wear a uniform. There was nothing now to differentiate them from other people. Each chose his own dress. When women were admitted to membership the variety became more marked. In the early days the members of the Community always sat together in part of the stalls. And great was the sense of achievement when at last the Community had so grown that at its annual regathering it occupied all the stalls on each side. But with the uniform this practice has gone too. The curious must look elsewhere and look deeper to find the indications of full membership of the Iona Community.

But despite the uniform there was nothing monastic about the new Community. Despite the job on which the members were engaged and despite the growing interest in the way of life of the previous occupants of the buildings, the Iona Community was not aiming at any mediaeval revival. They took no vows. The original members were all bachelors, but not confirmed bachelors. Most got married within a few years. While on Iona they lived a corporate, disciplined life. The ministers were committed to serve two years in a selected parish. This was seen as part of their training for their life-work. The purpose of the Iona Community was to provide training for work in the world, not to create a separated society. For this reason the original plan by which each man received £50 and all found each year was abandoned when the first batch left Iona at the end of the first summer. They went back to the ordinary conditions of work in Church and labour market. This was right. Otherwise members of the Iona Community would have become quite detached from the tensions of ordinary life. The Iona Community could not undertake responsibility, financial or otherwise, for members and their future families, even though some argued that it should.

Ministers and craftsmen were equal members of the Iona Community. But they were not treated equally. Only the ministers committed themselves for two years. But they were promised a paid job for these two years. On the island, in summer, labour dominated life. It was a hard lesson for the young ministers to learn. For years they had been students, doing what work they had to or wanted to do and at their own time. It was quite another thing to wait on the needs of others, to put up with all the digging and the carting and the waiting about before an actual bit of building was seen to be done. And perhaps the hardest part was to find that there was little to discuss with the craftsmen about the work. For the rest of the year, when members met in the cities it was the work of the ministers that was discussed. This was inevitable for only ministers were free to attend the meetings. And they had joined the Community for the sake of their work. The relationship of ministers and the craftsmen was difficult from the start. Indeed the tension lay at the root of the purpose of the Community. The craftsmen were necessary to the Iona Community and not just for building. The Community could not fulfil its purpose if it were just a community of ministers. But the craftsmen sometimes felt that, apart from their essential work, they were there to provide irritant raw material for the training of ministers. And they resented it.

But in creating this small community George MacLeod brought into being something that insisted on having a life of its own. He was, of course, from the beginning aware that this must be so. His talk at the time was all about community — the nature of it, the rediscovery of it and how it could be built up. He knew that it was a quest and a quest for something undefined and perhaps undefinable. And yet men must try to define it if they were to know what they were looking for. It was the consciousness of this universal and frustrating quest that gave the Iona Community its international links from the beginning. This is evident from a note on the back of the first issue of *The Coracle*: 'The Rev. George MacLeod is leaving early in November to fulfil an engagement made prior to the formation of the Community. It is to attend, as a representative of his Church, the World International Missionary Conference at Tambaram, Madras, India. He hopes very much that — in addition to the holiday it represents — he may be able to hear there of many efforts towards community that are being made all over the world.'

The pattern of the Iona Community's life was set in those first years by George MacLeod's clear vision and firm direction, by the influence of the island and by the sharing of work in fairly austere conditions. But the life itself and the way it was to develop were determined by the men themselves.

The Community had started as a brotherhood of ministers committed to serve in a parish for two years and of craftsmen who worked on Iona in the summer. At the end of the second year the first minister-members decided without any question and seemingly without much discussion that this could not remain the basis of membership. After the stipulated two years they stayed on as members. This became the accepted practice. The Iona Community did not become, as the founding document had seemed to forecast, a brotherhood of young ministers just out of college who stayed for two years with an equal number of craftsmen working on the rebuilding. This would have meant a constantly changing membership, with numbers not altering much from year to year and the balance of ministers and craftsmen remaining the same. It became instead an ever-growing fellowship of men who had shared life on Iona and were bound together by common concerns and a common discipline. The basic member was now the man who had been through the initial training and was now out in a job of his own. The man serving the first two years came to be regarded rather as a novice. And as new minister-members were added each year and craftsmen only occasionally, the Iona Community became predominantly clerical.

In taking this almost inevitable decision the members took the destiny of the Iona Community into their own hands and decided the way it was to go. Their decision brought with it a double question. What was to be the Community's attitude to those who still saw the Community in its first light? Theological students saw the Iona Community as offering two years of specialised practical training. Students from overseas wanted to profit from this experience. The idea of continuing membership was not something that they had contemplated at first. And what should be the attitude of the Community to those who after some years of active membership feel that they should drop out? In practice the Community has welcomed those who came in the first instance for the two years' practical training and has never regarded it as defection if a member after some years felt that he should retire. The Community thus became a voluntary brotherhood of men who renewed their commitment each year.

This inevitable but revolutionary development happened for three probable reasons. Firstly men had found together on Iona a kind of life that they had not known elsewhere. Secondly when they began working in their parishes they found the need of this relationship to support them in the odd solitariness of a minister's job. And lastly they had made friendships that they wanted to see last.

But this development in the life of the Iona Community raised another question: what was to be the pattern of life that was to bind them together? In the first summer on Iona the pattern had been obvious and simple: the corporate discipline of living together in one room, of common work and shared chores, of worship twice a day, of £50 a year all found. But this lasted only for the summer. When they scattered at the end of summer this discipline stopped. What was to take its place?

A new common individual discipline was worked out, mainly by George MacLeod. It had to do with prayer, the use of time and the use of money.

In prayer, each member was committed to keep a half-hour period each morning at 7.30 — of Bible reading, prayer and intercession for fellow-members and the work of the Church. This was easy to work out but not so easy to follow.

The use of time raised greater problems. They had shared a common time-table on Iona. They had together worked an eight-hour day. How were they to maintain a common discipline in the use of time when they went to their various jobs on the mainland? There was no problem for the craftsmen, if they were lucky enough to get a job. Their use of time was imposed on them. The ministers were a different case. According to the craftsmen they were going back to a one-day-a-week job. The craftsmen knew that the ministers would keep themselves busy for most of the time but the only times when they had to clock-in were the times of worship on Sundays. It was this freedom in the use of time that marked the difference between the ministers and the craftsmen. So to maintain some token of the common use of time that they had known on Iona, the Community adopted the rather artificial rule that its minister members should commit themselves to work an eight-hour day, by plotting it in the morning and checking it at night. This rule raised many questions, as, for instance, what counted as work, and which interruptions counted as having a prior claim? But it did keep the question of the use of time before the attention of members.

The discipline of the use of money presented even greater

problems when men went back to be paid the rate for the job they did. And the problems became more complex as men began to get married. It was one thing to have a little community of unmarried men, all of much the same age, all doing the same work for the same pay. It was quite another thing when the Community became a larger company of men, some married and some not, some with children but of varying ages and numbers, and working in a variety of jobs, no longer under the direction of the Community, with differing degrees of responsibility and differing financial rewards and commitments. This diversity of family life upset the simple pattern of devotional discipline. It raised new questions about the use of time. But, above all, it made a workable pattern of economic discipline very difficult to find.

It was to deal with this question that the first appointment to the staff of the Iona Community was made. Lex Miller had already been in close contact with George MacLeod and had been on Iona. He was a Scotsman, educated in New Zealand, where he had been secretary of the Student Christian Movement. He had come to England in the early years of the War and was Presbyterian minister in Stepney in the East End of London. The horrors of the blitz strengthened his pacifism and as a stranger not quite at home in England made him extreme in his Calvinism and in his revolutionary politics. It was not for this that George MacLeod invited him to become Deputy Leader of the Iona Community. It was indeed partly because of the agility and incisiveness of his mind and his ability to awaken discussion on political issues. But, more particularly, it was because he had definite views on economic discipline and personal experience of the operation of a particular scheme. He was a member of a small group of men and women, called the Shadwell Group because they worked in London's East End. The members were bound together by a commitment to live on the national average income, which at that time was £160 a year for a single adult. Those who

41

earned more put the balance into a common fund from which any member receiving less than the average was given enough to bring him level and from which grants were made for purposes approved by the group.[2] The scheme was a forthright experiment in economic discipline, based on the theory that the only income one was justified in spending as one's own was the average income of the nation. This figure was not the income of any particular person or class but a statistical figure calculated by the Treasury. The virtue of the scheme was that it took account of equity and gave useful experience in the corporate use of money.

In 1943 Lex Miller joined the Iona Community as Deputy Leader with the specific task of introducing a similar scheme of economic discipline into the Iona Community.

Lex Miller did much more for the Community than try to persuade it to adopt the Shadwell Group's scheme. By fierce and lengthy discussion and in practical experiment during the time of its tentative adoption the members of the Community were involved in an uncomfortable discussion of their personal finances in face of the economic position of others in the nation. The Community's romantic ideas were brought down to earth. At the same time Lex Miller's own form of political romanticism stimulated wider political thinking and prevented other members from following him blindly. In the field of political responsibility he made an effective contribution to the thinking of older members of the Community but his scheme of economic discipline, though adopted officially, never got off the ground. It failed basically because it was a scheme thought out by other people which the Community was expected to adopt in its entirety. It had not arisen out of their own discussions and experience. It also demanded a great deal of time to be spent in the keeping of accounts. This was all right for a group that existed for no other purpose. But

2. *The National Average: A Study in Social Discipline* (The Shadwell Group, St. Albans).

the members of the Iona Community had other things to discuss, many of which they regarded as of prior importance: their life on Iona, prayer and worship, the work they were doing in the parishes, the relation of the Iona Community to the Church of Scotland, pacifism, war. They were hesitant to commit themselves to living on the national average. It would be unrealistic unless their economic privileges were abandoned. This could only be done if the Community assumed responsibility for the economic future of members and of their families. And this would destroy any identification with other people. The Iona Community had always taken as its aim to find a way of life for its members which would have meaning for people facing the ordinary tensions of ordinary life.

But after Lex Miller's two years among them the question of economic discipline could never be disregarded by the members of the Community. Their rejection of the national average scheme of economic discipline forced them to look for some other more workable scheme which would express their economic interdependence and assist them to corporate responsibility in the use of money. They were not a group of men committed by vows to a life-long economic responsibility for each other. They had not renounced their individual responsibilities in family, work and society. Any scheme by which they learned to live better as workers, fathers and citizens must not cut them off from the problems and responsibilities of their neighbours.

It took some time to work out another and more suitable scheme. This was adopted in 1950 and is still in operation. It was in the first instance not worked out deliberately for and by the members of the Community. It was a scheme worked out by some members of the staff of Community House, led by my wife, for the staff and members of the House. So it was worked out in the setting of the Iona Community but for the needs of those who were not members. It was a simple scheme and easily operated. It was based on Income Tax returns. Income was taken as that recognised by the Inland Revenue. Allowances, income tax, rent and rates were deducted. The balance left was a man's disposable income. Of this, 5 per cent was paid into a common fund expended by the decision of members. The great virtue of the scheme is that it is objective and easily operable. It fails in taking no adequate account of differences of income. But it means that members are dealing with cash and not merely with theories. It forces groups — and such groups include wives — to take decisions about the use of money in the common fund. And such discussion leads into more difficult discussion as to how each spends the 95 per cent that remains to him. It is a token scheme. Its effectiveness as an educational process is proved by its continuance to the present day.[3]

This is to go beyond the early years. But the attempt at a common discipline is the main thing that holds the members of the Iona Community together and it is as well to discuss it together. For the intention of the discipline has remained unchanged from the beginning except that in 1967 a commitment to work for peace was added. This was to bring in another element: an addition to the earlier unstated commitment to mission and community. But the determining factors in any discipline, especially for a group of men who have not given up their individual responsibilities in family, work and society, are the use of time and money. We see this from the two unanswerable excuses that people give: 'I haven't time' and 'I can't afford it.' For time and material possessions are the only things that are ours to use. Our use of them determines how we live. In a convent or a religious order use of time and money is taken care of. In secular life they are matters of

3. See G. F. MacLeod, 'An Economic Witness by Churchmen', *The Coracle*, No. 18, April 1950. See also T. R. Morton, *The Household of Faith* (The Iona Community, 1951), p. 126, Appendix I, 'The Iona Community's Scheme of Economic Discipline'.

thoughtless convention or of every-day decision. In the discipline of a society like the Iona Community they must always remain central and matter for unending discussion.

The Community which George MacLeod called into being in 1938 grew into an organism with a life of its own. It grew in size because of the decision of its members to make membership a continuing commitment. It grew in size also because it welcomed young ministers from other churches — Episcopalians from Scotland, Presbyterians from Ireland, of many denominations from England, from Canada, Australia and always from the United States. And at the same time it widened its non-clerical membership to include others than craftsmen, so that it no longer talks about craftsmen but has to use that awkward word 'lay'. And in the seventies it welcomed women as members. Sometimes younger members talk, as if nostalgically, of the life of the Community in the days before they were born. If they were transplanted to those days they would not recognise the Community nor probably like it. If the first members could have foreseen the Community as it was to be thirty years on, would they have recognised it or liked it? This is only to say that the Iona Community is a living thing that has gone its own way. Doubtless it might have chosen a better way. But the composition of its membership, the experience on Iona, the work which they have themselves undertaken and, above all, the direction and impetus given to it by its founder set it on its particular way.

In this setting of its way the contribution of Iona has been very important. Iona not only gave the Community its name. It also gave it a local habitation. The members of the Iona Community could never have grown together to form a community if they had not had a place of work and meeting on Iona. It is not that they feel a special responsibility for the island, which is not theirs. It is rather that they belong together in an actual place of rock and sand, of animals and grass and growing crops, of storms and sunshine, of work and play. Like a family it has its roots in a place and memories.

Iona meant also commitment to a particular job of manual work. It is doubtful if the Iona Community could have survived the onslaught of war and the distractions of peace unless there had been the continuing work of rebuilding to draw it back each year to Iona. It was this demanding work that kept it from becoming too theoretical or too theological or too political. It could never follow to the end the leading of its excited arguments or change its programme each year to fit in with the views of its new members. The stage the work was at, the moving of stones and wood, the weather and the arrival or delay of the cargo boat decided the summer and the daily job. It was only when the work of rebuilding was completed that the Iona Community realised how much its life owed to the slowness of the work which it so often cursed, and how much it now lacks some demanding work on Iona to take its place.

The other determining factor that helps to set the line and keep the Community on it was the state of the contemporary world to which its members belonged. It would have been easy for them — and was often tempting — to draw a blue-print of what the Church and society should be like. But the place of work of each member was in the particular messy situation of parish, factory, school or office. The life of the Community was ruled by what was possible in life with those with whom its members worked. In this way Govan determined the life of the Iona Community as much as Iona did. Some complained that the Iona Community never got off the ground. It could also be claimed that it never got into the clouds.

CHAPTER FIVE

The Spoils of War

The Iona Community was cradled in war. Its infancy was lived not only amid the rumours of war but even more amid the facts of war. In this it was different from most of its kindred movements in Europe which were founded to help men recover from war and to face the facts of peace.

War carried the Iona Community into our modern world, as it carried the rest of us. It is idle to speculate on what might have happened to the Iona Community if peace had somehow been maintained. Results unexpected and important would undoubtedly have been achieved. But it was war that drew the unexpected lines that the Iona Community was to follow.

On Saturday, 2 September 1939, I left Iona early in the morning and travelled with George MacLeod across Mull by bus. With the outbreak of war almost certain I was anxious to get back to Cambridge. On the road along Loch Scridain and through the Great Glen, at every cottage — and most of the cottages now standing in ruins were occupied then — and at every road-end there was a man in uniform waiting in answer to his call-up. From Oban the train south was constantly delayed by trains going in the other direction with children being evacuated from Glasgow. In Glasgow the black-out was already enforced: no lights in the streets and people in their homes looking for black-out material and candles. I arrived at Cambridge too late for the beginning of the morning service at St. Columba's but in time to announce to the congregation that we were at war and to hear the first air-raid siren.

It was the end of an old, familiar way of life for all; an end to things that many took for granted and for us a recall to life as we had known it in China. It seemed to spell the end of so young and small a society as the Iona Community. How could it survive? Its members would be scattered. It could not expect students now to join. And was there any point now in rebuilding a ruined Abbey? It seemed the end of a short but pleasant dream.

But this was not what happened. George MacLeod was determined that the Iona Community should not fold up and vanish. The immediate tragedy only underlined the need of finding new ways of living in the world. The only way of bearing the present was to look to the future. Even the gesture of continuing building would give men hope. As he wrote at the time: 'The New Community for which the world is waiting' (and despite his confusing use of capitals he did not mean the Iona Community but the new common life that must emerge in the world) 'will never grow up over against, its emergence will be in and through, the present.'[1]

George MacLeod was confirmed in his intention by the support and encouragement of innumerable people of all sorts. Those who had been called up and had gone off to fight wanted to have some memory of hope to build on. Many of the clergy of all the churches knew that they would be tied to conventional jobs but wanted something to suggest that things would not always be the same. Unexpected people, in high places and in humble, wrote urging him to continue the work. A city base from which to continue the work started on Iona was provided in the Canongate of Edinburgh, when its minister, Ronald Selby Wright, went off as an army chaplain and the Iona Community undertook responsibility for the parish. The sending of men out in pairs to selected parishes was able to be continued with the offer of an interested friend to provide the money. George MacLeod undertook to send a

1. *The Coracle*, No. 3, November 1939, p. 17.

48

unit from the Community to serve wherever there was an emergency.

But it was the involvement of friends of the Community in activities on Iona that brought a new direction and a new dimension to the work there. The Abbey would have been left empty of men all the year round if they had not come to fill the void. Instead of the twenty men who had been expected to join the Community each summer, there was at best a mere skeleton of a team to carry on the work in a token way. One summer there were only George MacLeod, Bill Amos, the mason, and George Wilkie, then a student, now Industrial Organiser for the Church of Scotland. Progress would have been very slow if others had not come.

It was not too easy to come. All to the west of Oban and the Great Glen was a restricted area. Passports and permits were needed to enter it. The exigencies of war upset the plans of many. Catering was not easy, with rationing and uncertain freight and changing numbers. And it was not too comfortable when you got there. But men came gladly to help with the work. They knew that they were needed and they knew that they needed Iona. This work and this vision of a new life were shared by others than those living in the huts beside the Abbey. Visitors to the island and their children found satisfaction in helping. When supplies arrived all those available were needed at the jetty to unload the cargo.

What brought these others to Iona? The beauty and peace of Iona, almost incredible after the horror of the blitz and nights full of the noise of planes? Certainly this. The joy of building something however trivial against a world of destruction? As certainly. The pleasure of meeting unexpected people and of sharing a new kind of life in a strange place? Undoubtedly. And then there was the slow assimilation of the story of Iona, through centuries of achievement but more of disaster, back to Columba, who seemed to have something particular to say to us through the resilience that enabled him to live on Iona for thirty years, and through his sense of Christ's mission to other men and, as much perhaps, through that first industrial revolution of his which brought the horse and the plough and drainage to Iona.

Whatever it was that brought men during the war to Iona, and however varied the reasons, it was in the new work of rebuilding that they found satisfaction.

But their presence demanded a new programme. In the first two summers the programme on Iona had been devised exclusively for the new members. In 1939, in the summer before war broke out, lecturers had been invited each week to lead discussion with the new minister members. George Stewart, author of *The Lower Levels of Prayer*, and W. D. Maxwell, the authority on the worship of the Reformers, talked about prayer and worship. Jack Stevenson spoke about a rural parish. Eric Fenn, H. G. Wood and Roy Whitehorn, all from England, discussed the growing gap between Church and society. A few stray visitors appeared, including Marcus Barth, the son of Karl. But the programme was not for them.

The next year, 1940, the situation was very different. Instead of a constant group of twelve to twenty for the whole summer, similar in age, experience and intention, there was now a constantly changing succession of men of varying ages, occupations and experience who were involved in the work of the world as much as in the work of the Church. They came to Iona as individuals. But when they came they forged close links with each other and brought a wider life into the Abbey.

There was never any difficulty in arousing interest. When the first notice of the project appeared in a solitary newspaper article, George MacLeod received nearly a thousand requests for further information. By 1940 there were 2647 paid-up Friends of the Iona Community. It was from among these that summer visitors to the Abbey came. Among them were parish ministers ordained too soon to qualify for membership. There were others, ministers and laymen, who had worked with George MacLeod in other spheres of work. There were teachers and business men who felt that here there was something happening that they could understand and in which they could join.

It was for these men that the new summer programme was worked out in 1940. The members of the Community would regather on the island for the first fortnight of June. Thereafter 'from June 25 to September 10 a series of weekly "conference-retreats" will be held. . . . These conferences, commencing every Tuesday, are for men and special reference is made to those to which laymen are invited.'[2] The cost for the week, including travel from Oban and back, was £1.62. Two of the weeks were particularly for students.

This marked the beginning of what came to be known as 'Iona Weeks'. It also marked the beginning of the Associates of the Iona Community. Previously there had been the Friends of the Iona Community who supported its work and received news of it through *The Coracle*. The Associates went further than this. They shared in a common discipline and committed themselves to work for the same purposes as did the members. The Associates started with two specific groups which were composed of people who could not be members of the Community. First of all there were ministers of the Church of Scotland and of other churches, who were already engaged in work and were therefore unable to undergo the training for full membership. They saw the point of the Community. They wanted to help but they also wanted to gain what help they could in their own work. These formed the Minister Associates. Then there were women, ineligible because of their sex. They were as interested as the ministers, though not professionally. They were in a wide variety of occupations — teachers, doctors, deaconesses and many wives and mothers. Their interest was in the renewal of the Church and in the particular jobs and actions of service in which they were

2. *The Coracle*, No. 4, May 1940, p. 27.

engaged. In a quite particular way they looked for help in the discipline of their personal lives. Many of them had been brought up to regard prayer and charity as the tasks peculiarly laid upon them as women members of the Church but they felt that they had received little help in what to do with either. It was some time later, and after young people had insisted on being Youth Associates, that laymen felt that they too should form a more committed link. They came in later because, unlike the women, they could come to live in the Abbey and share in its work and because, unlike the ministers, they had no common professional interest to bind them together.

But the programme as it was worked out was not confined to Associates. There were, indeed, weeks specially for Minister Associates and for Women Associates. But these were outside the regular summer season, at Easter or in autumn. The summer 'Iona Weeks' were open to all men without exception and without regard to age, occupation, church affiliation or absence of any. In recent years, after the work of rebuilding stopped, residence has been open to women also.

These weeks have each had a particular topic with either a visitor or a member of the Iona Community as leader. But this discussion was not the main purpose of the week. Men did not come primarily to hear lectures or to take part in discussion but to share a life of work and worship, discussion and recreation. It was this, and particularly the ongoing and demanding work of rebuilding that prevented Iona from becoming merely a conference or retreat centre.

The development of the summer programme and the changes in the topics discussed indicated shifts in the interests of members and Associates but perhaps even more the changes that were taking place in the country and the world.

The first general summer programme, in 1940, had begun with two weeks for the Fellowship of Reconciliation with Charles Raven as lecturer. The only other visiting lecturer that summer was Dr. Karl Konig, founder of the Christian

Community at Camphill, Aberdeenshire, who spoke on 'The Church and Psychotherapy'.[3] One week was a Foreign Missionary Conference. Two weeks were work camps for students with Jack Hoyland, the Quaker from India and Selly Oak, as leader. The other weeks were led by George MacLeod himself.

When we look at the programme for twenty years later, in 1960, we find Charles Raven again opening the season with a week on 'Christian Ethics in a Nuclear Age'. He was followed by Leslie Hale, M.P. (now Lord Hale) on 'Politics, Ethics and Christianity'; by F. W. Dillistone, then Dean of Liverpool, on 'Symbols in Worship'; by John Wren Lewis on 'Science, Religion and Romance'; by R. D. Laing, of the Tavistock Clinic, on 'The Image of Man in Theology and Psychology' and lastly by Douglas Trotter, member of the Community, on 'Wholeness in Science and Religion: is a new Liberalism possible?' This list shows a development of interest in scientific and political topics of concern to all, lay and clerical alike. It had, for instance, become the practice to have, when possible, a Member of Parliament to discuss in practical terms a political theme and also to have a week particularly concerned with industry. In those latter years a new width in subject and method was introduced by means of weeks on drama, music and art. Sometimes these were as alternatives to the discussion programme. But sometimes they occupied every one. They did not take the form of lectures or discussions on the arts. They were action weeks. In drama those enrolling created and acted a play — all in one week. In music some piece was presented. In art, under John Busby of the Edinburgh College of Art, all who wished, including children, were given paper and paint and told to paint whatever they liked. The week was wet and the Abbey was

3. See article by Karl Konig on 'Integration' in *The Coracle*, No. 6, June 1941, p. 24; and on 'Integration in Medicine' in *The Coracle*, No. 8, January 1942, p. 19.

plastered with paintings of all sorts. All these weeks were not for specialists but for all who wanted to join.

If one dares to select those who in the earlier years made the greatest contribution to the thinking of the members and Associates of the Community — and the selection is bound to be personal — then the two that would stand out would be Charles Raven and John MacMurray. Charles Raven, Master of Christ's College, Cambridge, and for two years Vice-Chancellor of the University, combined a passion for pacifism with an interest as passionate in the birds and flowers of Iona and a keen political interest in world affairs. Visitors to the Abbey and young people in the camps were fascinated by his flow of words and by the new areas of experience to which he introduced them. John MacMurray, Professor of Philosophy in the University of Edinburgh, made, I think, a deeper though not a wider impact on the thinking of the members of the Community. This was perhaps because he was a Scot. It was probably more because his interests were more strictly political, economic and theological. Men listened entranced to Raven but were more stimulated in their thinking by MacMurray. What he was giving was what he had written in *The Clue to History*, published in the year of the Community's birth. In it he expounded ideas which, because of his presence on Iona, became embedded in the thinking of the Community in its early years and which in later years have been re-echoed by others as original thoughts. It was he who declared that the greatest contribution of the Jews to religion was that they abolished it. He emphasised the essentially political nature and implications of Jesus' life and teaching and so gave the members of the Iona Community solid ground for their political concerns. By his emphasis on, and use of, the word 'intention' he helped the Community — or at least some of us — to see that Christian obedience is never just a matter of theoretic acceptance of beliefs nor mere activism but something that holds faith and action together in life.

54

But if such visitors made an incalculable contribution to the life and thinking of the new minister members and the members of staff who were on Iona for the summer, their main audience was made up of other people. The group that they met in discussion was a heterogeneous collection of people, of differing ages, opinions, nationalities and churches. They were drawn to Iona not so much by the topic to be discussed or even by the fame of the lecturer as by the kind of life they were to share. Life on Iona was austere but enjoyable. It was life together with other people, with freedom to discuss and to think of the future. It was the horror of war that made it so acceptable. After the ruins of London, Coventry and Clydebank it was good to see some building going on. It was play, if you like: but creative play by which we learn how to live. Even today for many people the word 'Iona' recalls this free, enquiring life of discussion, work and worship which the summer programme sought to promote.

The war also brought young people to Iona. When the Iona Community began it had no particular place for adolescents or indeed for any other than ministers and craftsmen. But George MacLeod had long shown an interest in youth, especially under-privileged youth. And they were interested in him and in what he was doing. So from the very beginning young people came on their own to Iona in curiosity and hope. Doubtless something would have been done for them if there had been no war. But when war came and members of the Community were working in the east ends of Edinburgh and London, they became all too aware of the needs of young people in the shut-in society of a nation at war.

One of the first things that happened in the Canongate of Edinburgh when the Community moved in was the decision to experiment with some new kind of society for young people which would encourage initiative and responsibility, free from patronage and authority. George MacLeod and John Summers, who as a new member was working in the Canongate, set out to study the methods of 'Jeunesse Ouvrière Chrétienne,' a new Roman Catholic movement for industrial youth in Belgium and France, started by Abbé Cardin. They decided that this offered a pattern they could follow. The result was the founding of the Christian Workers' League in Scotland. This was certainly the only youth movement in Scotland at the time which was entirely governed and financed by its members and probably the only one that consistently did Bible study and followed a programme of action rather than of discussion only. The movement might have fared better today when we take youth more seriously. At that time it worked in too small groups, was too demanding of time and too slow in results to interest a Church and society that still counted success in big numbers and in quick results. It has now ceased to exist but in its day it helped many people and taught the Iona Community much. It also changed the face of Iona.[4]

Before the Christian Workers' League got properly organised the boys in the club in the Canongate insisted that they go to camp on Iona. This was during the war when tents were prohibited and only an old byre could be used. It was thought that the experience would teach them a lesson: they would find out that Iona was no place for them. Instead they taught the Iona Community several lessons: first that they liked Iona and the second that the Community must listen to their decisions. One was that regular camps for young people should be run on Iona for the full summer season. The other was that these camps must be for young women as well as for young men. The Community paid heed. Camps for young people were started the following summer and have proved perhaps the most effective piece of work carried out by the Community on Iona. From war-time onward the summer

4. See John Summers, 'The Christian Workers' League', *The Coracle*, No. 10, March 1943, p. 25, and George D. Wilkie, with foreword by George F. MacLeod, *The Christian Workers' League: a Movement for Industrial Youth* (The Iona Community, 1948).

programme on Iona, for members in training as well as for visitors to the Abbey, was always carried on in the midst of young people, sharing in the worship, asking questions, playing, shouting, irreverent, serious, shattering the complacent facade of church life and the peace of the island. It could be argued, but not proved, that of all who came to the island these young people were the ones most powerfully affected by life on Iona. Certainly they would make this high claim for themselves. What is beyond argument is that they made a contribution to the life that centred on the Abbey as great as that of any other group.

So round the tight, little community of full members the war brought another community, much larger, much looser, a very mixed assortment of men and women, old and young. It was indeterminate in limit. You could not say who belonged and who did not. Those who formed it varied in commitment. There were the Associates of the Iona Community who maintained a discipline and were kept in touch with the Community and with each other by a monthly newsletter. There were those who had made a personal commitment known only to themselves at the weekly Act of Belief. There were men who would never miss a week on Iona each year and never said a word as to what it meant to them. There were campers who remained in vociferous touch and those who disappeared until they came back with their children. There were hundreds who were on the files of the Friends of the Iona Community and hundreds more not known by name who still considered themselves to belong to Iona and Iona to them.

It was always good for members of the Community to be reminded that they had no squatter's rights on Iona. It was even more important for the Community to realise that in the end it was responsible for this endless stream of people. The Iona Community was not founded for its own good nor were the buildings being rebuilt for its own use. Its purpose was to help other men to find new ways of life for themselves by being willing to try to find them for themselves.

It was the war that brought so many people and made them so insistent. Doubtless without the war a wider community would have grown up around the community at the Abbey. Certainly the development of youth camps could not have been refused or long delayed. But an annual intake of twenty young ministers, as envisaged by George MacLeod and justified by the numbers then studying in the theological colleges — for 10 per cent of the output of the colleges in Scotland has been the average intake into the Community — would have formed a team large enough to provide all the labour needed by the craftsmen and to absorb the undivided attention of the staff and visiting lecturers. A few visitors would have been welcome if there was room, but they would have been there as spectators. Provision of a programme for them would have had to wait till the work of rebuilding was finished, the craftsmen gone and accommodation was available.

The war forced on the Community the early implementation of what it was bound ultimately to undertake: an experiment in adult education, even if it would never have described it as such. For the buildings they were working on would have to find a use. They would have to be used for and by others. Their ultimate use belonged to the unknown future. But the spoils of war laid down the inevitable lines of development. It was inconceivable that growth would alter the three principles on which this work for others was built.

The first principle was that Iona was open. It was open to all. There was no attempt to select or to screen those who came. Some weeks were, indeed, restricted to members of the Community, or to industrial men, or to students from overseas, or to associates, or to theological students. But many of these were outside the summer season. Generally the weeks in summer were open to men as residents without qualification of age, occupation or creed and to women living elsewhere on the island. Now with the completion of the rebuilding the weeks are open to women as residents. In this Iona is different from many other centres of laity education which run their courses primarily for selected groups, of particular profession, trade or interest.

Secondly, and because of this, the topics for the weeks were general rather than specific. They concentrated on some subject of common interest. They did not have to do with the particular interests of particular groups. Even when specific interests like drama, music and painting were taken up, the programme was not arranged for those with technical qualifications but for all who came whatever their knowledge, skill or ignorance. This was of intention. The particular interest of the Community was to help people to come to a fuller understanding of the Christian Faith and of their political responsibilities and of the inter-relation of the two. Politics and theology were, therefore, the two subjects that were basic to any programme. They are of common interest. They concern every one. They are also the subjects which we avoid whenever possible, especially in the Church. One of the easiest ways of avoiding them is to get involved in the discussion of sectional interests and activities. So we prefer to discuss the problems of some particular group — teachers or social workers or the poor, or what is wrong with the Church. The Iona Community has always felt that politics and theology are the two subjects that we neglect at our peril. Only when we are serious about them can we go on to consider sectional interests. The quest for the meaning of the Christian Faith for today and for the way of responsible action in the world was basic to the summer programme on Iona.

The third principle of this educational experiment on Iona was that the programme was not basically one of lecture and discussion. The 'week' was not a conference or a seminar. It was a week of shared work, worship and discussion. Work was

59

indeed the only obligation laid on a visitor. He went to worship if he wanted. He could skip lectures and discussion. But he had to do his share of work, on the building, in the grounds, or, more probably, in the scullery. This integration in life was as much part of the educational process as lecture and discussion. What is needed in adult education is close, informal, personal contact and the sharing of experiences which may be remote from the topic of the week. This was what made one of George MacLeod's most creative actions so important and so long lasting. It was called 'The Pilgrimage': a day's conducted walk round the island with stops for talks and worship at certain points and a longer stop for lunch. Visitors, campers, holiday-makers — all joined in. This natural and unforced meeting of people of all sorts in activity in the open air served many essential purposes of personal contact, free discussion and simple, united activity.

It may well be that this programme met peculiarly the needs of the post-war world. It was certainly designed to meet them. It offered a much needed opportunity for very mixed groups of people from many countries and of various church connections or of none, to meet together and to discuss the problems that faced them all. This is, of course, a constant need. But when life becomes more settled and organised, people are tempted to break up into specialist groups to discuss their own affairs and the basic questions of politics and theology are disregarded or discredited. Inevitably for the future new forms of programme on these open lines will need to be found.

Since the war the question of adult education has attained a new prominence, in discussion if not in achievement. We are only now beginning to recognise the nature and the size of the problem. Adult education is very different from the education of children. There can be no compulsion about it. In it we are dealing, not with other people, but with ourselves. It is not a matter of preparation for life, as we so often see education of

60

children and adolescents. It has to do with the life we are living now and the work we are doing.

What the Iona Community began to do because of the exigencies of war has been only a scratching on the surface. But the three principles on which its work on Iona has been carried out from the beginning stand basic to all adult education: the open door, the common topic and the sharing of life in some ordinary, intimate way.

The summer programme has now been extended well beyond the months of summer and takes in an even wider range of people. In particular it brings to Iona in other seasons very many more young people and some far younger people. It now depends on its own members rather than on visitors for the leading of its programmes. But the essential pattern has not changed. It was war's legacy.

CHAPTER SIX

The Challenge of Peace

War had brought to the life of the Community on Iona a new dimension and had set its programme on a new direction. But the war had highlighted social needs that had long existed but could no longer be ignored. The suffering of war and the hope of peace engaged men in large scale planning and made them ready for deliberate experiment. Plans for the Welfare State were already in preparation, under Lord Beveridge. An inclusive scheme of national social insurance and a national health service would soon be enacted. The war had in particular unmasked the needs of young people. The government initiated a Youth Service which laid responsibility on the local authority to care for the needs, social, educational and recreational, of young people outside school hours and after they had left school.

The Church shared in this urge to make new plans. The Church of Scotland had its commission on 'The Will of God for Our Time', which advocated the public control of the means of production; and a later commission on mission — 'Into All the World' — which envisaged new forms of witness and service for the Church. Of all the government's plans probably the one that raised most question in the Church was Youth Service. Before this the service of young people, outside school hours, had been left to the churches and the voluntary youth organisations. It was now recognised that the task was too big to be undertaken by them alone. A national service had to be planned to cover all young people and not just a privileged few. The churches were naturally a bit suspicious. They were afraid that their position would be challenged. They also feared, with justification, that the programme of the official Youth Service would lack content. It could have nothing to do with religion and politics. And so it would have nothing to say about faith and action. It would tend to be purely recreational. At the same time it could not be said that the churches were doing very much about faith and action, at least so far as young people were concerned. It was a very uneasy situation. Everyone realised that there was a lot that had to be done but no one was clear what to do. It was a situation that certainly called for new ways and fresh experiments.

Where did the Iona Community stand in all this? Much of the planning was in line with the Community's own ideas and discussions. Indeed the Iona Community could be seen as a small prophetic movement pointing the way to greater things. But the community might well have held back from any official involvement if it had not been, as it were, catapulted into deliberate experiment, to the bewilderment of its members but to George MacLeod's gratification. In 1943 an anonymous gift of £20,000 a year for seven years (later extended to ten) was offered to the Youth Committee of the Church of Scotland for experiments in youth work along the lines of the Iona Community. The gift was gratefully accepted. The trust deed which was the vehicle of the gift expressed the conviction 'that the future welfare of the people of Scotland is bound up with and dependent upon a reassertion of Christian conviction among its youth and the practice of the Christian Faith in terms likely to call forth from them discipline and devotion'. It also desired 'that the essential principles of the religious body known as the Iona Community be applied to the wider work of the Church of Scotland and that Iona itself, insofar as convenient, be felt as the inspiration of these methods'. The work to be undertaken was more particularly specified as 'to support training centres for teachers and youth leaders, to help to establish experimental centres of religious teaching in industrial districts, to finance summer camps, particularly on Iona, and generally to stimulate activities among young people, including those who would be demobilised when the war ended'.[1]

The source of this generous gift remained a secret for quite a few years, except, of course, to those intimately concerned. It was, in fact, made by Sir James Lithgow, Bt, shipbuilder and Scotland's leading industrialist, regarded by many as a reactionary capitalist but the first practical supporter of the Iona Community, and by Lady Lithgow who shared his interest in Iona and who was herself actively engaged in the work of youth clubs.

This gift meant that at once and perhaps without adequate planning practical schemes of experimental work had to be set in motion. But before anything could be got going, an organisation had to be devised, some definition of principles accepted, a programme adopted and staff selected.

Trustees were appointed, representative of the donors, the Youth Committee of the Church of Scotland and of the Iona Community, with a Policy Committee responsible for the practical direction of the work. This committee had a wider representation and included the members of the staff.

According to the trust deed the lines of work were to follow the essential principles of the Iona Community. These had never been precisely defined. The Community had been started in the belief that in action things would become clearer: that those who did the will would learn the doctrine. Now a little more definition was needed. So, to explain what the essential principles of the Community were George MacLeod wrote a book — *We Shall Rebuild*, published in 1944. Its publication was a considerable achievement at a time

1. J. M. Reid, *James Lithgow: Master of Work* (Hutchison, 1964), p. 218.

64

when paper was strictly controlled and when no publisher could be found to undertake the work. That it was published at all was due to the enthusiasm and publishing experience of John Morrison. He set up the Iona Community's own publishing department to bring it out.[2]

In the book the principles of the Community were not put down in any propositional form. Instead it described in pictures the problems that faced Scotland and the world and gave an indication of the changes needed in the life of the Church to enable it to fulfil its mission in the post-war world. Priority was given to the recovery of lively corporate worship. This led into the necessity for political action and economic witness. The congregation as the agent of mission was emphasised and the way of its working explained in terms of experience in Govan. Then followed an account of the Iona Community and its rule of life for members and Associates. The book is, indeed, more a programme of action than a statement of principles. It was all the more readable on this account. It had a very wide sale and did much to publicise the Iona Community.

As the Trust was of limited duration there was need for quick action in devising the programme. Inevitably it bore the marks of urgency, hope and uncertainty, inspired by relief at the approaching end of the war and by the recognition of the need to find new ways to meet the problems of peace. In this it was typical of many war-time social enterprises and of the many more that followed with the coming of peace. It was not heroic like Cimade, the French Reformed Church's organisation for war-time relief and post-war reconstruction, with which we had close contact in those early days. It was not so ambitious and high-powered as the Evangelical Academies started in Germany a few years later to help lead the way to

2. George F. MacLeod, *We Shall Rebuild: the Work of the Iona Community on Mainland and on Island* (The Iona Community Publishing Department, 1944, reprinted 1962).

democratic life there. It felt a specially close kinship with Agapé in Italy. But like all these movements it saw its task as immediate and urgent.

The purpose of the Trust was not specifically to support the Iona Community nor to serve the Church of Scotland. Its purpose was to serve young people. To this end four lines of action were selected.

First, new work was to be started in three selected depressed industrial parishes to meet the needs of young people through a positive programme of life and action. Two of these parishes were in Glasgow. These were The Barony in the centre of old Glasgow and Overnewton farther west, behind the Kelvin Hall. The third was the mining parish of Fallin, near Stirling. These experiments followed the lines already used in Govan and, perhaps more fully, in St. Francis-in-the-East in Bridgeton, in the east end of Glasgow, where a new kind of church life had been started by Sidney Warnes and developed by Arthur Gray. This work was based on the conviction that congregation and parish must be one: that the church was there for those in the parish and not for a congregation gathered from outside. The work in the new experimental parishes ran into difficulty because the attitudes of the congregation and of the youth of the parish did not agree. The work in these Glasgow parishes has come to an end, as much as anything because the parishes have ceased to exist through the demolition of old buildings and the creation of new roads. This was always to be expected. But lessons were learned. Perhaps the main lesson learned was that something more fundamental was needed in the life of the church if it was to serve the inner city.

Secondly, the Iona Youth Trust took over the responsibility for the youth work which the Community had started on Iona. Property on the island was acquired, equipment was purchased and staff increased. This enabled two camps in the future to be run concurrently during the summer so that twice as many young men and women as before could come. A salmon fishing station on the north shore of the Ross of Mull was rented so that a more adventurous kind of camp could be run for groups of boys, including boys from Borstal. When the Trust came to an end this extended work was handed back to the Iona Community and has continued to be one of the most effective bits of work carried out by the Community. To this the Trust gave both means and impetus.

Thirdly, a small residence was opened in Glasgow for men coming back from the war who wanted to enter the ministry of the Church. This never came to much, probably because not enough thought was given to the radical changes needed in theological education. It was probably also not sufficiently related to the practical work of the other experiments.

And last, though primary in planning, was the opening of Community House in the centre of Glasgow. It was not named and was never intended to be called 'Iona Community House'. The name 'Community' was chosen to emphasise what it was trying to offer — a place where men and women could meet and talk and, hopefully, find community for themselves. It was chosen to indicate the fundamental nature of the questions they would inevitably discuss: the problem of living together and with all other men and the difficult steps that had first to be taken. It was not intended to give what we now call a community service. It was not meant to serve those living in the immediate neighbourhood. Indeed the site was chosen because there were few residents in the area. It was central and accessible from all parts of the city and surrounding towns. Of all the work undertaken by the Trust it was the most experimental, the most controversial and the most expensive.

It was for Community House that the first appointments to the staff were made. Before there was any house and while it was uncertain whether if a building was found we would get permits to transform it, my wife and I were asked to come north from Cambridge to share in the planning and running of it. There was no doubt about the uncertain nature of the appointment. As George MacLeod warned in a letter in the early summer: 'BUT, face the fact that we may not get the permits for transforming things: and you might be so landed for a whole winter or for the whole war.' But he gave some definition of the job itself: 'You would be chaplain to the chapel in the place, host to the canteen, organiser of the Book Department (a difficult but imaginative job) and above all thinker out and organiser of the classes to be held in the place. . . . If I know anything about the show so far your work will never be defined. . . . I should imagine one of your jobs at the beginning would be to travel England and find, from other church organisations, HOW NOT TO DO IT.' This letter was followed a week later by three post-cards, mainly taken up with sketch plans of the proposed house, but also saying: 'The Committee unanimously decided to ask you both to come as from Oct. 1. We will offer £350 to you and £250 to Jenny.'

We accepted, despite the uncertainties, because the challenge of a new enterprise appealed to us. Also the idea of a joint appointment. The place was to be a house and not an institution. We would be living in it with our children as part of it. To our mind it had to be a joint appointment. Jenny, with her experience in India and China, in Cambridge and in broadcasting, had a definite contribution to make to the policy as well as to the life of the house. In any case she was taking on responsibility for the design and furnishing of the house and in particular for the design, equipment and staffing of the restaurant, which was seen as central in the whole programme of the place. This all seemed self-evident for a house that was to be for women as much as for men. We did not realise how strange the whole idea was for Scotland. Among the members of the Iona Community there was suspicion and even resentment at a woman being allowed to occupy a responsible position. The Church of Scotland were correct and even cordial in their welcome. I was made an honorary member of the staff of the Youth Committee and attended their committees and staff conferences. Jenny was one of the very few women appointed to the commission on evangelism which produced the report 'Into All the World'. Of course our experience had been in China and in England, and the experiment was strange and uncertain and seen by some as a criticism of the ordinary work of the Church. In any case we had to do with the Iona Community. So suspicion, as well as curiosity, was the natural reaction, in a society as masculine as the Iona Community and the Church of Scotland.

It was an exciting, if frustrating, adventure. The first winter was spent in waiting for the building to be purchased and then waiting for planning permission to make alterations, in discussing with the architect, Jack Coia, about the plans and also in planning for the programme after the House should open.

The House was definitely to be for youth, though the definition of youth was wide. It was not for children but for adolescents and young adults. It was for those who had left school and were going out into adult life. It was for those coming back from war service either to a civilian job for the first time or to an old job in conditions radically changed. In a more particular way we were looking to that great army of young men and women who were running the juvenile organisations in the city and its surrounding area. All these young men and women were in their different ways looking to the future with great hopes but with many questions about what life and service would mean in the world that was so hopeful and at the same time so terrifying for us all. Two questions from two pamphlets published in 1944 may indicate the mood in which we entered upon the task and the way we talked about it.

'The call to the service of youth arises from the sense of the need of the youth of this country. We may express the need in various ways. We may talk about the break-down of the old social solidarity of family, village and shop. We may talk about a failure in education. We may talk about the disruptive influences of war and of new economic conditions. But, in the end, we mean that we live in a society which has largely cut itself off from its traditions, which has discarded its old religious and social sanctions, which no longer regards a knowledge of the Christian faith as necessary or relevant to life. That is: we now live in a secular society. That is something quite new. We who are older do not see this strange new world in all its starkness because we see also all the time the little stable world we have made for ourselves. But for many youths on leaving school it is the only world they do see. They come up against it in a way we can never come up against it. For youth sees it in all its novelty and in all its difference from the familiar attitudes of school and home. That's why youth is in conflict. That's why there is a problem for youth as there never was before. It's not that boys and girls are in themselves any different, but that their position is. The problem is not in them but in society. The world they are called upon to enter is not for them an inheritance they enter upon in hope, but a jungle. They are, as it were, the inhabitants of a new continent, a continent that is strange and pathless.'[3]

The second quotation, taken from the first booklet describing the purpose of the House, takes up the same theme but develops its religious implications.

'Youth feels that he is entering a land whose only maps are out of date and which is in no sense his own. Of this he is aware. But behind this there is a more fundamental lack. He might not be unduly worried at living in an age when accustomed things are in dissolution, if it were not that the unquestioned postulates of the imagination have also failed him. It is from these that spring the feelings of wonder and awe, of fear and joy. It is through these that man knows his place in nature and his separation from nature; through these too that he knows his place in

3. T. Ralph Morton, *Missionary Principles for the Home Front* (Iona Youth Trust, 1944), pp. 2, 3.

family, community and nation. And it is through them that his understanding of the meaning of God develops. It is these that are taken for granted all through the Bible and all through the centuries of the Christian era up to our own. It is possible to see in science and in art a search for new postulates of the imagination. But in youth who are not consciously searching there is evident the same hunger. This can be seen both in the fear of any of the simple emotions and in the fascination for such a manifestation of the simple emotions as they see in Russia today. And so behind their sense of the unreality of the social structure there is a much more fundamental sense of the lack of the reality of God. And that sense of the unreality of God which is expressed by many youths outside the Church is also evident, even if unexpressed, among many inside the Church. But it is not based on intellectual reasoning and cannot be met only by such. It goes much deeper.'[4]

It was to meet this situation that the House was opened. Its purpose was educational. It was there to give a place to young men and women, and to those not so young, where by discussion, study and action they could begin to find a way for themselves in the post-war world. Despite the pessimistic diagnosis of these quotations, young people were not then pessimistic. They were not looking for some sign of hope or some task to do. They were almost blindly optimistic and anxious to serve. But they did not see how to do what they wanted to do. They did not know on what they should build their hopes. The House was to be, in some sense, a city counter-part to Iona, to the camps and conferences and the worship in the Abbey, but with greater emphasis on study, discussion and action.

In the middle years of the forties there was no difficulty in making contact with people. There was a surge of desire to find ways of life and service with little enough available in the way of excitement, interest and training. When the House opened, long queues formed outside to attend the guest-

4. *Community House 1944* (Iona Youth Trust, 1944), pp. 6, 7.

nights at which the purpose of the House was explained. Men and women enrolled in the courses by the score.

Before the House opened up plans had been made for these courses, with a time-table and programme and helpers found. The four main subjects had been decided by George MacLeod. They were described in the wording of the time as 'The Meaning of the Faith', 'The Faith and the Social Order', 'The Use of Drama' and 'The Use of Films'. The first two were inevitable. The inclusion of drama and films was due to George MacLeod's appreciation of the importance of the visual arts and of the mass media and of the need of participation in action to balance discussion. Four courses, one in each section, were to be held on four evenings of two ten-week terms, one in autumn and one in spring. All attending were to share each evening in some kind of joint activity and in worship.

But little could be done without additions to the staff, and nothing at all in drama. Nothing could be done there without the right professional man. We were very fortunate in finding him through the interest of Bill Smellie of St. John's, Perth, and of Frank Shelley of the Perth Repertory Company. I travelled to Hastings through a snow storm to meet Oliver Wilkinson and his wife and wondered much more anxiously whether I should get back safely than whether they would come. But he accepted the offer at once and with enthusiasm. Probably he did more than anyone else to make the purpose of the House visible to many.

The time was opportune for drama in Glasgow. There was great interest in acting. And there were few to help with new ideas and professional service. The School of Drama at the Royal Scottish Academy of Music was not opened till some years later. The Citizens' Theatre under John Casson and the Theatre Workshop under Joan Littlewood were exciting many people. Community House was one of the few places where amateurs could experiment with drama and where professional help could be given in the practical matters of lighting, make-up and production.

But this was not the main work that Oliver Wilkinson did. He saw drama as not only the reproduction of other people's plays but rather as the creation by a group of their own play and then their presentation of it. The first play publicly produced was based on George MacLeod's book *We Shall Rebuild*. It attempted to present its basic ideas on the stage. Inevitably it was more of a pageant than a play. It was produced in one of Glasgow's theatres with a large cast. A fuller example of group creation was the dramatisation of the account of Paul's visit to Philippi as told in the sixteenth chapter of *Acts*. A group of thirty-four people, by no means picked, discussed the incidents with open freedom and with Uist Macdonald to deal with any difficulties in the text. Then when a play had been bit by bit written, read and discussed, torn up and written again and again, it was presented on the stage with a cast of thirty-two people who had been active in its creation. They included John Grieve, now well known in TV and on the stage, and John Gibson who later joined the drama staff of Community House and then became a drama producer with the B.B.C. The play was thought to be good enough, or interesting enough, to be published by the Religious Drama Society, with a preface by Martin Browne, a full description by Oliver Wilkinson of the making of the play and an appendix of practical notes on production.[5] The play was effective but the main effect was on those who created and presented it rather than on the audience. But this was the purpose of the exercise. Drama was seen as a means of education through discussion which had to be free, through literary composition which few realised that they were practising and through the release that acting brought to many.

Such work involved a great many people: in writing, in acting, in staging, in making costumes, in building the lighting

5. *The Journey* (Religious Drama Society, 1949).

equipment. People were learning to do things together and were enjoying it.

But there was also the use of drama in propaganda. The House, through other courses, was trying to get people interested in local politics. Drama was used to bring this concern on to the streets. Simple plays were presented from a lorry at selected and permitted vacant sites in the inner city, with previous noisy tours round the immediate neighbourhood to draw the crowd. This led to plays being taken out to churches and village halls on tour.[6]

When Community House was opened films seemed as important a means of communication as drama. The cinema was booming. Amateurs were interested in making films and in showing them. In co-operation with the Scottish Religious Film Society the House ran courses of training in projection, made modest attempts at making short films and discussed film appreciation. But the tide soon began to ebb. Television was taking over.

One of the fundamental aims of the House was to encourage social and political action among young adults. At the end of the war men were, on the whole, aware of the magnitude of the political problems that faced the world but reluctant to be involved in political action apart from voting in the general election of 1945. There still prevailed the strong conviction that Christians should not get mixed up in politics. This was the legacy of the First World War. Before that, from the time of the Reformation, members of the churches had always been involved in political actions. The break came when the issues changed from ones like Ireland and education, which seemed to call for moral judgments, to economic ones on which Church people had not been trained to think at all. They gave up any attempt at moral assess-

6. See Oliver Marlow Wilkinson, with foreword by Dame Sybil Thorndike, *First Report of Experiments in Drama carried out in Community House* (Iona Youth Trust, 1946).

ment of economic issues and settled down to attend each to his own economic advancement. So religion and politics were for the first time separated, at the very moment when Christian insights were most needed. This was the problem that Community House faced.

At first we had to tackle it ourselves, with the help of many visiting specialists. The first need was to get discussion going on the immediate questions before men's eyes — industry, housing, local government. It is hard for us now to realise how novel a subject for discussion industry was and how unwelcome to many. My wife, as joint-warden, stimulated interest by arranging visits to ship-building yards, engine shops, etc., and by getting people to discuss industrial questions from opposing points of view. In one very lively course George Thomson, then a Glasgow editor and later a Commissioner of the European Communities, and T. R. Craig, then chairman of Colvilles and later a director of the British Steel Corporation, met with a group each week for ten weeks to discuss industrial problems, from opposite points of view but in perfect amity. Hugh Gibson, who had joined the staff, arranged courses on all sides of local government, at which members and officials of the Corporation gave information and debated their policies. Emphasis was on the burning issue of housing. Exhibitions of new housing plans, including models of the first multi-storey flats, were staged in the House. To help people to understand how local democracy worked, three wards were selected for people to work in at election time, each choosing the party for which to work.

Other means were used to encourage discussion on wider issues. Weekend conferences were held in the House. One of the largest and fiercest was on the plans for the National Health Service. Residential weekends were held in hostels outside Glasgow. One, on communism, was attended by over a hundred young men and women.

In all this work the Youth Committee of the Church of

Scotland co-operated through Alice Scrimgeour, clubs organiser, and David Orr who, on leaving the army, was appointed Senior Youth Organiser and took up residence with his family in the House. He involved young adults of the churches in Glasgow in 'action groups' in Community House. These followed the methods of study and action pioneered by the Christian Workers' League. By this means close contact was gained with the youth of the Church. It was also the means by which the experimental work of the House was seen as linked with the on-going work of the Church.

All this took place in the early years of the House. The development of this side of the work needed someone of political knowledge to give his full time to it. We were fortunate in finding Penry Jones, then on the staff of the Student Christian Movement, and inducing him to join the staff of the House. In 1951 he added to the scope of his work by becoming also industrial secretary of the Iona Community. His coming led not only to more systematic teaching on politics but also to regular conferences on industry, to the formation of industrial groups in a number of parishes, to a regular industrial week on Iona and to the inauguration of a scheme by which theological students, men and women, of different churches, lived for a summer in Community House, going out by day to work in local industry and in the evening discussing the issues raised. It can be claimed that his work led to the initiation of industrial work by the Home Board of the Church of Scotland.

This freedom of discussion and this interest in political questions attracted to the House from the beginning many individuals and groups committed to political action. A Youth Parliament met in the House, composed of the youth sections of the various political parties. Through this many who are now national political leaders, such as Bruce Millan, Gregor Mackenzie and Dickson Mabon, became well known to many. Politics was in the air. It was also on the ground.

76

We would have said that the fundamental courses in the House were those on 'The meaning of the Faith'. We certainly still thought that this could be dealt with as a separate subject. At the beginning the courses on this subject were well attended. But even then it was obvious that many of those who enrolled were more interested in how to teach the faith to others — Scouts, Guides, members of youth clubs and so on — than in what it meant for themselves. Probably this interest in practical matters was intuitively right. We cannot usefully discuss faith in the abstract, apart from what we do and say. The meaning of the faith can be understood only in the unity of life and action.

This unity could not be very obvious in the programme of the House with its separate courses. But it was visible in the structure of the House itself. When the Trust purchased the building, it was a warren of small workshops, offices and a large wholesale ladies' clothing warehouse. Jack Coia, the architect, transformed it into a visible unity of work and worship. The work was done towards the end of the war when permits for building were hard to obtain, the amount of money that could be spent severely limited and materials difficult to come by. So the result was austere. But it spoke its message. The House was to be as wide open as possible and to be seen to be open. It was to be a place of meeting and not just a place where meetings could be held. So you entered straight into the restaurant which had plate-glass windows on to the street. When you came in the kitchen was open on one side and the chapel on the other. My wife had great difficulty in persuading even the architect, and much more the contractors, that this was what we wanted. They submitted about the chapel, though they thought it odd that we did not want to be quiet. But they were convinced that a kitchen should be kept out of sight, but we got our way. The idea that work, worship and life were a unity and must be seen as such was novel then, and even shocking. But the idea of openness went farther; there was to be no door dividing off the wardens' flat from the rest of the House. There were to be no notices saying 'Private'. It was to be a house, not an institution. Unexpected people wandered up to the flat at night and we had many thefts. But if you call a house 'Community House' it must be open and be seen to be open, intellectually and physically. This visible openness was probably the most effective teaching that the House offered on the meaning of the Faith. Today with new architectural ideas and greater freedom in construction we might have built an entirely different style of house. Perhaps we wouldn't have had a chapel at all. For even having a chapel implies division. But, on the other hand, if you are trying to demonstrate a desired unity you need to indicate the divided things that you are trying to bring together. At the time when Community House was opened work and worship and life were seen by most people in the Church as distinctly divided from each other. They still are and we don't achieve unity by ignoring divisions.

It was an exciting experiment and perhaps it was over before we knew that it had begun. We thought we were trying out things when we should have realised that we were doing the things themselves. But this is probably of the nature of all experiments. The test comes when serious thought has to be given to the form of its continuance.

The House might have developed quite differently if there had not been tensions that often came near danger point and that blew up in the end. A venture financed by one group (the Trustees), directed by a combination of this group and two others (the Youth Committee of the Church of Scotland and the Iona Community) and carried out by a staff on the principles of the last was bound to run into difficulties. Trustees — who give or hold the money but are not engaged in the work — are probably not the best people to be responsible for an experiment. The Trustees claimed that all that they wanted to do was to provide the tools and let the staff get on with the job. But it never worked out like this. They were suspicious of the political activities that went on in the House though they never questioned the staff's policy of allowing expression to all views. George MacLeod was perhaps in the most difficult position of all. He was a trustee. He was the director of the policy of the Trust. He was the author of the principles of the Iona Community. He was under pressure from all sides and in a very equivocal relationship to the staff of the House. Were we colleagues? Fellow members of the Iona Community? Or employees of trustees who met behind closed doors?

The position was further complicated at this time by a controversy between George MacLeod and the Courts of the Church of Scotland. From its beginning, and despite the blessing given to it by the General Assembly, there had been continual and, on the part of some, fierce discussion as to the constitutional place of the Iona Community within the Church of Scotland. There seemed no place for a religious community, and much less for a religious order, except as a private society. And the Iona Community was not just a private society. It went to the theological colleges and recruited men. It appointed young ministers as assistants to parishes at its own discretion and of that of the parish minister. And now through the Iona Trust it was acting in co-operation with the Youth Committee of the Church. And yet it had no place in the courts of the Church and the courts of the Church had no control over it. To those interested in the law of the Church — and most Presbyterians are constitutional legalists — there was room here for endless controversy, even among those who supported the work of the Community. The General Assembly appointed a succession of committees to study the question and report and their reports led to the most lively of discussions in the Assembly. While this problem showed no sign of being solved, George MacLeod was asked by the congregation of Govan Old Parish to go back as their minister and he expressed his willingness to accept the call. This would have entailed his giving up the active leadership of the Iona Community though he would have retained authority as founder and plans were being discussed about future organisation. The Presbytery of Glasgow decided after long discussion that as he was the leader of a movement outside the jurisdiction of the Church it could not sustain the call. The case went to the General Assembly of 1949. The Assembly ruled against him. The affair shook George MacLeod by its assumption that the Iona Community had nothing to do with the Church of Scotland and by its seeming questioning either of his wisdom or of his loyalty.

But the decision also shocked the Church. On the motion of Dr. John Whyte the General Assembly appointed a committee to consider a plan to bring the Iona Community within the jurisdiction of the Church and to report the next year.

The last years of the forties were, therefore, a time of great strain and uncertainty for the Iona Community and for the Iona Youth Trust and not least for the experiment of Community House. It was not a situation in which new lines could any longer be followed light-heartedly. But despite the strain and the personal tensions that it brought, it must be said that all the time we were convinced that the House had been set on the right lines. It was thrilling to live in the very centre of Glasgow, to look over the forgotten river to the staid terraces of the Gorbals and to watch small steamers unload sand and gravel opposite the House. Above all we knew and our children knew what a stimulating and satisfying thing it is for a family to grow up in the place of their parents' work, with daily contact with all sorts of people, with no privacy indeed but with the joy of sharing in adult activities. This made the frustration only the harder to bear. We could not but be aware of lost opportunities and of uncertainty about the future.

The uncertainty of the future was the final point of division between the staff of the House and the Trustees. The Trust would shortly come to an end. But the work would have to go on in some form. And this would involve the staff — or a staff. The staff could not help being concerned about plans for the future of the House. If the House was to continue — and if the present staff was to continue — then serious thought had to be given to plans for the future programme and finances of the House. The position then became so difficult that my wife and I resigned as wardens of Community House in 1950.

I did not resign from the Iona Community. And, indeed, shortly afterwards George MacLeod asked me to act as deputy leader. We moved to Edinburgh for a year and it was then that Candlemakers' Hall was taken over as the office of the Community. In addition to help with the administration, I was asked to undertake two particular duties. One was to get the economic discipline scheme working for members and to introduce the idea to the Associates. The other was to write a small book to explain the reasons for economic discipline in the Church. This was published in the following year under the title *The Household of Faith*.

By this time the situation had become very much easier. The General Assembly of 1951 decided to bring the Iona Community within the jurisdiction of the Church. It did so by setting up the Iona Community Board as a committee of the General Assembly. The Board reported to the General Assembly on the work of the Community and the General Assembly could instruct the Board. But the General Assembly and the Board had no responsibility for the finances of the Community. The Board saw its task as acting as a means of communication between the General Assembly and its Committees and the Iona Community and not as that of directing the work of the Community. As a very adequate safeguard of the freedom of the Community the General Assembly decided that the majority of the members of the Board should be nominated by the Iona Community and that

George MacLeod, as Leader, should be the Convener of the Board. So the bitter controversy about the constitutional position of the Iona Community in the Church of Scotland was ended. The Iona Community was recognised as being within the Church. Its staff were regarded as the servants of the Church with the same standing and duties as the officials of other Assembly committees. At the same time the liberty of the Iona Community was maintained, including its right to have within its membership those of churches other than the Church of Scotland. It should be added that recently and at the suggestion of the Community the practice of the nomination by the Community of the majority of members and of having the leader as convener has been abandoned.

At the same time the Iona Youth Trust was coming to the end of its existence. Community House in Glasgow and the camps on Iona were handed over to the Iona Community. This made planning for the future possible and I came back to the House as warden. But this was too late for some of the work to be recovered. The Iona Community took over responsibility, questioningly rather than enthusiastically. It has taken many years for the members of the Community to realise the opportunities as well as the problems that they have inherited in Community House and in the camps on Iona.

This deliberate experiment of the Iona Youth Trust obviously raises many questions. But awkward questions may be as useful fruit of an experiment as easy visible success. Some of the questions are, no doubt, due to the peculiar situation of the Iona Community and of the Iona Youth Trust, particularly in relation to the Church of Scotland. But some are common to all enterprises founded on money from outside sources, dependent on a specialist staff to carry out their purposes and which interpret these purposes as service of other people. Most new experiments operate on these conditions. How many can do anything without money, staff and a programme? The hospitals, universities, medical schools and colleges established by the churches and other organisations in Asia and Africa depended on lavish grants of money, the appointment of highly trained staff and a carefully worked out programme. The post-war institutes of laity education in Europe, the industrial missions in Britain and America, all depend on money from somewhere, a trained staff and a programme. It is easy to see the weakness of the method and the difficult questions, both immediate and long-term, that it raises. But we have yet to find how to get on in any new experiment without money, staff and a programme.

These questions attain a new urgency when the founder retires or the original gift of money comes to an end and when new men have to justify the continuance of the work to a new generation and to find new means of support. How does the enterprise pass from the experimental to the accepted stage? How does it do so without losing vitality and drive? The enterprise may be under church control and liable to changes in hierarchical authority and, in times of financial stringency, to crippling economic cuts. It may have its own trustees or board and be dependent for finance on business interests that limit its freedom. Power may be vested in the staff or at least in a responsible leader and the enterprise may therefore be at the mercy of the policy or the health of one man or his successor. These are the reasons why some experiments have not lasted or have run into serious trouble after twenty years. How are these difficulties to be avoided? Can they be overcome? Or is there some other possible structure for such experiments?

Community House had its troubles. Its achievements were not slight. It showed the possibility of new lines of action in Church and society. It demonstrated the value of a house in the centre of the city open to all, welcoming to new ventures, however suspect they might seem to some. But perhaps its greatest achievement is quite beyond measure — in the men and women who have disappeared into the wider world to love their fellows with some kind of new vision and understanding.

And Community House has survived to find quite a new life and a fresh purpose in a new generation. It has survived and been able to develop along new lines because of its incorporation in the Iona Community. It enjoys a continuity denied to many of its contemporary movements. This continuity is expressed, not in money and in the staff, but in the members of the Community. It is this that gives any enterprise connected with Iona its uniqueness. It may at times slow down the speed of the experiment. It may at times seem to be bogged down in unending discussion. But the continuity of the Iona Community prevents the collapse that other experiments have shown. It assures its future.

CHAPTER SEVEN

Second Generation

Continuity has been the secret of the Iona Community's life. Its continuity has been that of an ever changing membership. In this it resembles a family rather than an institution. A new venture that is started to meet some particular need, such as a school or a hospital or an industrial mission, generally starts with a founder of vision and drive and a team of enthusiastic younger men with some sort of supporting body in the background. Staff come and go but the pattern remains. And it is the staff that gives the continuity. The Iona Community might seem to the casual observer to be of this pattern. Its founder certainly set it on its way and maintained its drive. But the abiding and peculiar and sometimes frustrating nature of the Iona Community lies in its membership, which is rarely visible as an entity to those outside. It is its membership that ensures continuity, for the members make it a community and keep it so.

It is its continuing and ever changing membership that prevents the Iona Community from being simply an institution with staff, and makes it something much more difficult to define. It is a society with a membership constantly changing in number, location, work and relationship to each other. It is in this like a family. It has some younger members under authority; and some who rebel against the customs and tradition of the family. Most of its members have grown up and become responsible members of the world outside. They run their own affairs and may not often be seen at home. There are a few who have to take decisions and act in the name of the whole. They all try to come together on occasion to demonstrate and celebrate their unity. For they are sustained by the sense of belonging to each other and are aware of a common way of thinking about things and of doing things. They feel themselves all members of one family.

But the parallel between the Iona Community and the family is not complete. It is not by birth or marriage that a man or woman becomes a member of the Iona Community. His entry is not dependent on someone else. It is of his own choice. In this it might be said to bear some resemblance to a religious order. But he takes no vows nor does he give up his secular responsibilities. It has rather an odd resemblance to the freer communities of the later Middle Ages, such as that founded by Gerhard Groote and often known as The Brethren of the Common Life, of which one of its leaders wrote: 'We are not members of an Order, but religious men trying to live in the world.'[1]

It is perhaps more like a scattered congregation, with members of various ages, except the very young, all engaged in their own particular jobs and with their own family and other responsibilities, some of them living and working in other countries, but all united in affection and in a common intention and meeting together when they can. I don't imagine that the members of the Iona Community ever think of themselves as such a gathered congregation of a rather exclusive kind. But this is a fairly adequate description of their way of life. It is not surprising that this should be so. The idea of the congregation has been a determining factor in the thinking and in the work of the Iona Community from the beginning. The Iona Community was born out of George MacLeod's experience in Govan in the years of the depression. His

1. Quoted in R. W. Southern, *Western Society and the Church in the Middle Ages* (Penguin, 1970), p. 344.

experience resulted in the recognition of the failure of the congregation as the agent of mission in the parish and of the need of its recovery in some new form to meet the needs of industrial Scotland. Indeed the acceptance of the parish as the proper and inevitable area of the Church's mission implied the acceptance of the congregation as its instrument. It is significant that in the early years when some new idea about the work or discipline of the Community was suggested, the determining question was whether it could be applied in a congregation. If the answer was clearly 'No', then it was not for the Iona Community either. It is therefore not surprising that the Community which was so aware of the problems and opportunities of the congregation should display some of its forms and some of its tensions.

The family and the congregation have peculiar and similar tensions which the institution does not know. These tensions are, in the main, due to the differences of age, occupation and experience among the members and to the fact that a member cannot easily be got rid of. The staff of an institution have their own tensions but when these become critical they can be resolved by changing the staff. This solution is not open to the family nor adequate for the congregation. Because of this the family and the congregation are always aware of the tension between the generations and the conflict of interests of those who are preparing for their life-work and those who have settled down to theirs. The Iona Community shares this tension.

It was not till the fifties, when the Iona Community was nearly twenty years old, that characteristics of this family or congregational pattern became apparent. Up till then the Community had seen itself as a group of rebellious young men prepared to go out into the world to find new ways for Church and society. By the fifties it knew itself to be a society of varying ages and of diverse experience, many of whose members were already in responsible positions in the world.

The realisation of this came late and rather suddenly. The old pattern of the leader and a group of young followers continued unquestioned during the war, when numbers were few. After the war numbers jumped up with the return of men from the forces to begin or to complete their college courses. The number of those who joined the Iona Community was large and spread over several years. The men who joined were older, with a wider knowledge of men and the world, than those who joined in the first years. But they joined as men learning a new job and as men with experience of one kind of training who knew that they lacked training in another. While in training they did not question the old pattern. They expected to receive disciplined training as they had received it in the army. But when they went out to their own jobs they quickly reverted to the authority and leadership that they themselves had exercised during the war. And inevitably they attained more quickly than their earlier fellow-members to positions of responsibility in the Church and in their local communities. They became the dominant members of the Iona Community in the late fifties.

The members of the Community were aware that the Community was changing. They tended to see the problem as one of size. Was it becoming too big? Was it losing the intimacy of the original small band of men all of an age? Should it restrict its membership to so many a year? Or should members retire after a fixed number of years to keep the age-level down and to prevent the domination of seniors? And what about lay members? The number of craftsmen was limited by the work to be done on the rebuilding; should other kinds of laymen be recruited to maintain some kind of balance? And if so, would not this make the size of the membership quite unwieldy?

Size did, indeed, raise problems. It became difficult for the member, apart from the leader, to be sure that he knew all his fellow-members even by sight. Some were abroad and some were prevented by their jobs from regular attendance at meetings. But size brought compensating advantages. Scattered members were often not so isolated as they had been before. In any region of the country there were likely now to be several members who could meet together. So size made possible the development of local family groups of from six to ten members and their wives. This brought a new intimacy and informality into the life of the enlarged Community. But there was the danger of it becoming a collection of groups and losing the sense of a larger fellowship.

The more serious problem that growth brought and size represented lay in the new range of age and greater diversity of experience of the members. Members could now be divided in age by the difference of a generation with all the years between represented. There were the men just out of college. They knew little of the beginnings of the Community. It was something that they took for granted as belonging to the background of their lives. They had plenty of questions to ask — about how the Community functioned and what was expected of them. There were the others — the great majority — who had been in the Community for five, ten, or twenty years. Their questions were very different and arose out of the nature and problems of their jobs. But they all, young and old, apprentices and veterans, were members of the one community. Their attitudes, experience and expectations were very different. And some of them were in a peculiar relationship to others. In particular the youngest and some of the older members were working together in the often difficult relationship of assistant and parish minister. This range of age and this diversity of experience brought to the Iona Community greater change and greater challenge than did mere size.

This attainment of a second generation brought with it also a change of interest. When asked, as we were continually,

'What does the Iona Community do?', we no longer pointed to Iona as the easy illustration of the Community's work. We said that what the Iona Community did was what its members were doing, all over the place, in their parishes and in their secular jobs. But this was not ever so easily described. Every man's job was his own and different. And none was done in the name of the Iona Community. It was done in the name of the local church or the school or the office or the business. The Iona Community could not either claim the credit or take the blame. But it was still what the members of the Community were doing.

The Coracle, the journal of the Iona Community, began to be more concerned with the varied work of its members than with the work of its staff on Iona. The issue for December, 1953 (No. 24) is noteworthy in that it is the first issue not to carry a photo of Iona — indeed, no picture at all but instead on the cover the signatures of all the members of the Community. It also had no news of Iona. Instead the opening article, by John MacIntyre, then Principal of St. Andrews College, Sydney, and later to be Principal of New College in the University of Edinburgh, was on 'The Theology of Community'. It was followed by descriptions of the work of members in six parishes all different in type, of the work of the Iona Community with men in industry and of the work of a member in India.

At this time the experience of members working in Asia and Africa and elsewhere overseas was making a contribution to the life and thinking of the Iona Community out of all proportion to their numbers. This was partly because they were working in conditions different from those at home but which yet revealed in an acute and rudimentary form the problems of industrialisation with which we were all too familiar in Britain. In particular the inevitability of political involvement and the essentially corporate nature of the Church could not be disguised overseas by ecclesiastical conventions. Also, those abroad were clearly acting on their own and often seemed to have an authority and independence denied to those working in familiar conditions at home. Almost certainly the contrast was exaggerated. The position abroad was probably never so dramatic as those at home liked to think. Nor were those at home so much the victims of circumstance as they themselves liked to think. But certainly those abroad seemed to be doing what those at home wanted to be doing. Their contribution to the Iona Community at this time was very great.

But new things were happening at home, particularly in the parishes. When at the beginning, in *We Shall Rebuild* George MacLeod expounded the aims of the new community, he did so in terms of the renewal of the parish. In the fifties this was still the dominant idea. When members talked about experiments it was to experiments in the parishes that they usually referred, not to what was going on in Iona or in Community House in Glasgow, or in the youth work or incipient industrial work of the Community. This was partly because the great majority of members were working in parishes. It was also because new things were certainly happening there. The most conspicuous of these experiments was 'The House Church'. The experiment had found its prophet, exponent and teacher in Ernest Southcott, then vicar of Halton in Leeds, who made the idea of the House Church known throughout the Western world. Coincidental with his activities similar experiments had been going on in parishes in Scotland. Close contact was made and maintained with Ernest Southcott. In *The Coracle* of 1953 descriptions were given of experiments in Burntisland with David Orr, at St. Ninian's, Greenock with Bill Cattanach and at St. Martin's, Port Glasgow, with George Wilkie. *The Coracle* for March 1956 carried a leading article on 'The House Church: the next step? or a first step?[2] Two further pamphlets

2. T. Ralph Morton, 'The House Church: the next step? or a first step?', *The Coracle*, No. 28, March 1956, p. 1.

described the experiment.[3] The work continues but in changing forms. It has had an enlivening effect on the life of the congregation but cannot be said to have renewed it.

The point to notice is that these experiments were being made by members of the Iona Community on their own in their own jobs. They owed little to decisions of the Community or to suggestions of the staff, though, of course, they owed much to general discussion among the members. It was inevitable that as members gained wider experience and greater responsibilities some of them should want to try new ways and right that they should work their new ideas out on their own in their own places of work. The Iona Community had come into existence precisely to encourage such activities. As years passed the work that members were engaged in became more diverse. Now in the seventies we are confronted with a list of occupations which is as wide as it is intimidating: and this despite the number of senior members who have withdrawn from active membership because they felt that their immediate commitments were too demanding. The list includes university professors and lecturers, the principal of a church college, lecturers in colleges of education, university chaplains, headmasters, social workers, hospital chaplains, doctors, a lawyer, an architect, a member of staff of the British Council of Churches, as well as the great majority in parish work and the minority in industry. This is a very different community from that of the early years when it was composed of young ministers and craftsmen, all much of an age. Diversity of responsibility has been superimposed on the basic common experience of youthful training. The demanding commitments of middle age come in conflict with the wilder enthusiasms of youth. This diversity of activity and concern has greatly enriched the life of the Iona Community but it has brought its problems. It is understandable that some have

3. George D. Wilkie, *The Eldership* (The Iona Community, 1958), and David C. Orr, *The House Church* (The Iona Community, 1961).

found themselves so committed in time and concern to their responsibilities outside the Community that they have felt it only right to resign from full membership. The Iona Community in this reflects the problems of the congregation which thinks it knows what to do with people in training but fails to support those who are engrossed in the work of the world or to bring their wider experience back into the life and thinking of the Church. How does the width of experience of older members of a congregation relate to its life and worship? How do the activities of senior members of the Iona Community in their jobs and in their other concerns relate to its domestic life and to what goes on in Iona? The two questions are basically the same. It is doubtful whether the Iona Community has so far brought forward any answer to help the congregation.

This urge to be involved in outside jobs and concerns was due to the teaching and emphasis of the Iona Community from its beginning, and in a very particular way to the ideas and example of its founder, George MacLeod. The members of the Community were 'religious men trying to live in the world'. The needs of the world were always dominant. But in the fifties the demands of the world pressed with peculiar force upon its Leader. Perhaps the refusal of the Church to let him go back to Govan made him restless for wider horizons. Certainly when he was offered appointment as the first Harry Emerson Fosdick visiting professor at Union Theological Seminary, New York, he had no hesitation in accepting. In the autumn of 1954 he went to America for the academic year. After his return, in 1957 he was elected Moderator of the General Assembly of the Church of Scotland. This meant that for a year he was deeply involved in travel at home and abroad on behalf of the Church of Scotland. Then, in 1958, he accepted the convenership of the Church Extension Committee of the Home Board of the Church of Scotland with the express purpose of wiping out the accumulated deficit of

£400,000. This kept him very busy with duties outside the Iona Community for another two years. Thereafter he gave a great deal of his time and attention to pacifist propaganda and to a host of outside engagements.

His appointment as Moderator was a recognition of his personal achievements and of his work in the Iona Community. It was warmly welcomed by its members. His other activities were in line with all that he and the other members of the Iona Community had advocated in social and political involvement. But these activities and those of other members of the Community raised questions as to what the Iona Community itself should be doing in this second stage of its life. What does such a community do when it has got beyond the stage of seeing its primary job as that of training its young members and is essentially a group of mature men active in the world?

At the time the problem found expression in the discussion as to whether the Community had a line and what that line was or should be. It had been easy in the early days to talk about the Community's line. It could point to the corporate training of young ministers with craftsmen in work and worship. It stressed the need for the recovery of some kind of corporate devotional life. It advocated the use of the congregation as the agent of mission in the parish. It insisted on the necessity of responsible political action on the part of Christians. This line in the first few years could be followed by all the members. But when there was growing diversity in the activities and responsibilities of members it was much more difficult to impose a line that could be followed equally by all. Was the line to be something that men in training would be expected to follow? Was it the policy to be followed in work for which the Iona Community was directly responsible on Iona, in Community House in Glasgow and in the youth work? Were the members of the staff the only members committed to follow the line of the Community? If the line was to be followed generally by all members of the Community, would it not be in danger of ending up merely as a devotional discipline or the proclamation of agreed opinions? These incessant questions could never find satisfactory answers and led to a good deal of frustration.

This growing involvement of George MacLeod in important activities outside the Iona Community necessitated changes in its administration. When he went off to America for a year I was appointed Deputy Leader of the Community. I had, indeed, been combining the wardenship of Community House with the Deputy Leadership. But now I ceased to be warden of Community House and became full-time Deputy Leader. This was in reality a new kind of job. The job I had been doing as Deputy Leader had been done previously by others. Lex Miller had acted first for two years. After him Archie Craig on his retiral as the first secretary of the British Council of Churches acted as Deputy Leader for one year, before going back to Glasgow University. Then Robert Craig, now holding the unenviable position of Principal of the University of Rhodesia, served for two years. Their job had been to assist George MacLeod in the administrative work of the Iona Community. The job I now took on was rather different, at least in its first year. When George MacLeod left for America he said to me: 'Just carry on as if I were dead.' Of course I did not take this seriously. I kept him informed about what was going on and asked his advice. But it was my responsibility to see that the work of the Community was carried on and, if possible, developed without worrying him too much. The work of rebuilding had to be pressed forward and the inevitable emergencies dealt with. A particular responsibility was to see that the rebuilding of the Michael Chapel was finished by the date fixed for its opening. The monthly meetings of the Community had to be planned and conducted; also the regular monthly meetings of the Associates in Edinburgh, Glasgow, Aberdeen and Dundee.

The theological colleges had to be visited. Recruits had to be interviewed and their placing in parishes arranged. The summer programme for them and for visitors on Iona had to be prepared and publicised. In addition there was the editing of *The Coracle* and of the monthly *Iona News*, attendance at innumerable committees and many outside arrangements.

It was bound to be a strenuous year. But its beginning was made much more difficult by two unexpected and unfortunate events.

The first was, indeed, tragic. George MacNeil had been Secretary of the Iona Youth Trust. After his retiral from that office he had been secretary of the Pearce Institute in Govan. In the summer of 1954 his body was found in his flat in Govan. Murder was certain and a former Borstal boy who had disappeared was suspected of it. He was extradicted from Spain and tried and found guilty. The Iona Community was deeply concerned because of its relationship with both the victim and the accused. George MacLeod flew back from California to give evidence. Rumours were rife about the kind of people with whom the Iona Community was connected. But comfort was found in the attitude of some in authority. This was perhaps best exemplified in a letter from the Moderator of the General Assembly of the Church of Scotland:

'Dear Mr Morton,
    I write a note to say with what sympathy and admiration I have regarded the Iona Community in the sad trial occasioned by the recent case in the Courts. I expect Dr MacLeod has returned to the U.S.A. by now. Perhaps you would let him know how proud we in this house — and we represent many — were of the way he acted and spoke. May I also add that the letters, etc., in the Press by yourself and Dr MacLeod were, in our view, most admirable. I should like to pay a humble tribute and to subscribe myself, with kind regards,
                    Yours sincerely,
                        E. D. Jarvis.'

The other event was merely unfortunate. James Maitland had resigned his parish in Edinburgh to become Warden of the Community House in Glasgow. After his appointment and while on Iona he took very critically ill and had to be rushed to hospital. It was some time before he could take over his new duties.

These two events cast a shadow over the year. They made serious planning for the future impossible and the carrying out of routine jobs difficult. But in the midst of the worries and uncertainties of the time there was an occurrence that was both distracting and significant. My wife, who had done a lot of broadcasting in England and was at the time engaged in university missions in Scotland and in England, was involved in a radio discussion on Religion and Morals with Margaret Knight, the evangelist of old-fashioned fundamentalist humanism. It is difficult for us today to appreciate the commotion this controversy aroused. The programme was a London programme and Scotland was not supposed to be interested. But so great was the interest in Scotland that radio programmes in Scotland had to be altered to give space to this London event. The biggest Press conference so far known in Britain gathered to interview the two debaters. The national Press gave it full coverage. Publicity even spread to America where the affair was fully reported in *Time* magazine. The correspondence that flowed in on my wife was overwhelming.

The whole affair was a welcome distraction amid our troubles. It provided cheerful publicity for the Iona Community when so many strange rumours were floating around. It was significant because it revealed new interests and questions. It was significant too in that it aroused fear and suspicion. There was resentment in broadcasting circles at great popular interest in a religious discussion and a resolve that it should not be repeated. Certainly this discussion between Christian and humanist was never followed up. What was more surprising was that the Iona Community never cashed in on their opportunity. Did this intense popular interest mark the end of an epoch, the last spasm of an old controversy? Or was it an indication that we were moving into a time of greater openness, when men asked old questions but wanted new answers? The pity was that Church and authority avoided the issue.

Certainly this time of critical happenings and of new questionings marked a definite stage in the history of the Iona Community. It had moved from the primary to the secondary, from being experimental in its training of its new members to leaving its older members to be experimental in their own jobs in the world. George MacLeod's growing involvement in outside affairs was typical of this shift of interest. But perhaps more significant was the adoption at this time of Penry Jones, the Community's industrial secretary, as Labour candidate for the constituency of Berwick and East Lothian. He fought two elections unsuccessfully and then embarked on his outstanding career in television, with both I.T.V. and B.B.C. Responsible political action and use of the mass media were what Community House had been advocating in word and teaching. It was good when a member of staff decided to act.

The Iona Community had passed through the novelty and excitement of its beginning. It had survived the romance of Iona. It had found its recognised place in the Church of Scotland, while retaining its freedom to be open to those of other churches. It had established the fact that the life of its members was in the world. It faced a choice of ways. It could see its task as completed with its members sent out into the world to serve with commitment and hope. Or it could welcome a problematical future knowing that it must find a new life for itself and a new purpose for its members out in the world. It must, in other words, accept the known or seek the unknown.

This 'second generation' stage is the critical one for all experimental movements. They have justified their initial actions. They have been accepted. Others see how they can be used, but only if they remain as they are. To get on to a new stage is very difficult. Such action often seems to supporters to be an abandonment of what has been achieved and won approval. To those who are engaged in the experiment there comes the shock of realising that they must again accept doubt and uncertainty. For the second stage, though necessary, is still untried.

This was the crisis that faced the Iona Community in the fifties and has remained with it. The Community was not ready for it either through its organisation or its experience. The near completion of the rebuilding on Iona tended to make the members think that the problem was one of organisation and of changing programme. And indeed the end of the work of building was to bring difficult problems of adjustment and policy. But the real problem went deeper. How were the members of the Community in their variable and responsible jobs in the world to make a corporate contribution to the life of the world while maintaining their individual freedom? And how was the inner life of the Community to be organised to help them in this, without cutting them off from the life of other men? It is doubtful whether the Community as a whole then or since has given its corporate thought to this. But how do you do it? Nothing is more certain than that by concentrating on the state of a society or a party or a church and attempting to define a new purpose, confusion and uncertainty and questioning so take possession that nothing can be decided. It is often only by having to deal with a difficult practical problem that the way forward is found.

Fortunately the impetus of the enterprises to which the Iona Community was committed and the demands of its Associates and Friends kept the staff of the Community too busy to worry and indeed forced it to find new ways of working.

One thing that was achieved in the year of George MacLeod's absence was the formation of a finance committee which should control the Community's income and expenditure. Up to this time financial responsibility had been in the hands of the Leader and the Trustees. There could be no development of responsibility for its own future unless the Community not only knew about its finances but had control of them. The committee had as its convener Ian Reid, who later was to succeed George MacLeod as Leader. Without this pedestrian but necessary step the Community could not have begun to plan for the future.

During these years some new developments took place. The orientation of the programme on Iona veered a bit away from the inner life of the Church towards concern with what its members were doing in the world. This is seen, for instance, in the conferences on Iona for the summer of 1957. These included J. A. T. Robinson on 'The Christian Doctrine of Matter and Power', Sir Leslie Plummer, M.P., on 'The Problems of Emergent Nations', Professor James Barr on 'The Economic Teaching of the Old Testament', John P. Mackintosh on 'Domestic Political Problems', John Wren-Lewis on 'Christianity in a Scientific Age' and W. H. Hamilton on 'The Community and the Child'. The shift of interest was evidenced in the complaint of some members that not enough ministers were coming to Iona. Lay people were more in evidence. This had been our intention and hope.

The Iona Community had always been interested in men's jobs: with what they did and not just with what they said. In the early days George MacLeod, using Johannine language, was fond of saying that it was only in action would we learn the truth. But in the first two decades of the Community's life it was with the jobs of ministers that it was almost exclusively concerned: with what they should be doing in the parish and how they should learn to train themselves and their congregations for the work of the parish mission. The craftsmen were with them on Iona but no-one dared to discuss their work.

From its beginning the Iona Community had been concerned with men in industry. It was realisation with shame of the Church's failure to men in industry that moved George MacLeod to resign his charge and set up the Iona Community. But the problem that the Community faced was that of the mission of the Church in an industrialised society — the need for change in its way of life and, in particular, the need for change in the training of its ministers. It was not until 1951 that the Iona Community began to think of industry and not just the Church's mission to industrial men. A committee was appointed, of which I was chairman, to consider action in the field of industry. This led to the appointment of Penry Jones as the Industrial Secretary of the Community, while still remaining on the staff of Community House in Glasgow. His work focused attention on the secular work of men and on the ethical, political and theological questions that industrial life raised in itself. This work took the form of the organisation of groups of industrial men in some parishes, the holding of industrial conferences in Glasgow and of industrial weeks on Iona and of contact with industrial experiments elsewhere and, in particular, with the Sheffield Industrial Mission in its pioneer days under Ted Wickham.

Interest in industry was not confined to the manufacturing industries of central Scotland. It was recognised that agriculture was the biggest industry in the country and that it raised problems as acute as those in any other industry. For some years agricultural conferences were held in Perth.

From the very start of its concern with industry the Iona Community was convinced that industrial mission must be the work of the whole Church and not of a group within the Church. The Iona Community was therefore glad and gratified when the Home Board of the Church of Scotland set up their Church and Industry Committee and appointed as its secretary George Wilkie, a member of the Community. This meant that the Iona Community no longer undertook industrial mission on its own. It did not mean that the Community gave up interest in the work. It continued to supply full-time members of staff to the Church for this work.

This wider concern with the work of men in the world found its main forum in the monthly meetings of the Community and naturally affected its general thinking. But it also involved the contribution of many outside the full membership of the Community and especially of its Associates. In particular it led to the formation of a group of Men Associates. Up to this time the Associates had been divided into Minister and Women Associates and Youth Associates. What bound the Minister and Women Associates to the Community and to each other was a common interest in devotional discipline and in the work of the Church. The new group of Men Associates shared this interest but with an overriding concern with their jobs and with the question of their Christian obedience there. Because of this they were far more radical in their criticism of the Church's current life and theology. They were never large in number. And they were all professionals — professors, lecturers, teachers, social workers. They had their own economic discipline, insisted on their members taking part in some form of political or social work outside the Church, and circulated among themselves reports of what they were doing. They also met regularly in residential conferences.

The Men Associates were keen to break down the division between Minister, Women and Youth Associates and to have only one kind of Associate. This was done. But it is doubtful whether this was a wise step. Once the groups gave up their special interests, what bound them together was what was common to them all — devotional discipline and an interest in church work. What suffered was concern with their outside jobs, which were different for each. The Associates have certainly continued to grow in numbers and obviously find satisfaction in being associated with the Iona Community and with each other. But perhaps one of the greatest failures of the

Community is that it has never provided the free and open development which Associates have always been seeking. There have been great difficulties. The Community has never been in a position to provide a member of staff solely for this work. There is the question whether they should not provide their own leadership. And finally there was the almost inevitable ignorance of the ordinary members of the Community as to who the Associates were and what they were doing. They were the bridge of the Community into the world but few seemed anxious to cross it.

This new emphasis on the secular jobs of men, illustrated in the emergence of the Men Associates, was probably more clearly to be seen in new developments in the youth camps on Iona. They went far beyond the Abbey programme in departure from clerical themes and in open concern with the ordinary questions of young men and women in industry and society. They had to. The first account of the youth camps ever to appear in *The Coracle* was in the issue for November 1958, twenty years after the founding of the Iona Community. In this article John Jardine, who was then Youth Secretary of the Community, wrote this about the programme:

'It is easy enough to get some people to talk. It is more difficult to ensure that the same people are saying what they really think. It is often a Herculean labour to get the people who can say the vital word to open their mouths. And in Iona with such a rich gathering of people sharing life it is important to give them an opportunity to share their thoughts. In recent years one of the most exciting things about the youth camp has been the way in which developing techniques of discussion have been worked out. The basic purpose has been to try to get people to say what they really think, either by direct or indirect means. A favourite method is to ask people to take on the role of someone else and, in thinking themselves into a stranger's position, they often reveal to themselves facts about their own.'[4]

4. *The Coracle*, No. 33, November 1958, p. 17.

The work on Iona for young people was later further widened by Jim Robertson, when he was Youth Secretary, through the development of activities for those at school. A pioneer experiment had indeed been made a few years earlier, when in May 1960 a party from Dennistoun Junior Secondary School in Glasgow spent a week in the Abbey. It was composed of twenty boys and twenty girls, all fifteen-year-old school leavers, and was led by Mrs Jenny Morrison, the Lady Superintendent. A description of the visit, written by her, appeared in *The Scottish Educational Journal* and was reprinted in *The Coracle*, No. 38, for March 1961.

These school weeks were not vacation camps for children on holiday. They formed part of the regular curriculum of the school, organised by the school, financed by the relevant Education Committee and led by members of the school staff. They proved so popular that the difficulty was to fit in all the schools that wished to participate. Classes that came were mostly of those about to leave school, but junior and senior groups also came and from schools of all sorts. The great value of these weeks lay in the novel experience of corporate life and in participation in the life of a small adult community, mainly of craftsmen, and in the life of the island. For the children shared in the work of the Abbey, domestic, gardening and where possible building and on the crofts. This was very different from living in a hostel. It was a real insight into island life and adult life as well as close acquaintance with birds and beasts and flowers. It was exciting and gratifying for city children.

This activity with school children led to a growing interest in the Colleges of Education in what was going on in Iona. The great extension of the programme on Iona which now ran from March to October was mainly due to the development of work with youth, from junior school children to university students. This work was probably the most useful of all the Community's activities on Iona. It was probably the most far-reaching in results, though these can never be measured. And in the growing concern with the secular life of the world, including the life of its members in the world, work with young people was fundamental. For young people are the essential laity.

But between this youthful activity on Iona and the work of the members in their parishes and other jobs there was a considerable gap. It was a gap of communication, in information and in interest. It was not that those on either side of the gap were in any sense in opposition. They were intent on the same aim. But they never seemed to make contact with each other. This was a pity, for the camps were more experimental than the members realised. And the work of members in their parishes and secular jobs was often more experimental than they admitted or sometimes realised. This gap in communication between the work of the staff and the work of the members was different but parallel to the gap of the generations between the members. But both these gaps indicate, not failure, but growth. They inevitably belong to a living organisation, whose members are growing older and moving out into bigger jobs and wider responsibilities. They present difficulties and challenges and raise many questions. But these are the difficulties and questions of life rather than of an experiment.

At its start George MacLeod often talked about the Iona Community as an experiment. It was to try new ways. It could take chances not open to the Church. It could dare to make mistakes. This was its justification. And new ways were needed and the courage to make mistakes.

But the language of experiment is difficult for a body that begins to find its own life. We tend to use the word 'experiment' rather loosely. Perhaps we should use it only of those enterprises that are undertaken to test a theory or to gather statistics. The Peckham Health Centre was such an experiment. No one questioned the value of the service it rendered to people. But when the information wanted was collected it was closed down. Its purpose was a printed report not a continuing work. The Iona Community was not experimental at all in this sense. It was indeed started with the intention of trying new ways and was prepared to find that some worked and some did not. In this sense it was prepared to be experimental. It was experimental in the sense in which life is always experimental. All life's most worthwhile activities are undertaken without experience, for the first time — being born, getting married, begetting a child and even going to school and entering a job. The essence of these experimental actions is that they commit to continued life. If the Iona Community was trying to do anything new it was committing itself to continued life — to new tensions and unanswerable questions. After twenty-five years the Iona Community was ceasing to be an experiment of youth and was entering into adult life.

The temptation was to want to get back to the simplicities of its youth — to have a line, to work on a plan, to know exactly what it wanted to do, to be a success. But as a member of the Community was to write in a later issue of *The Coracle*:

'There is a hellish craving for success in the Church which I take to be a sign of utter divorcement from reality. The more you have a clear plan, scheme or programme, the greater the divorce. The truer the Church, the more confusion it can bear. We are not half confused enough.'[5]

Members were worried about a line or its absence. Others, more objective, were asking: What was the Iona Community doing? What had it achieved?

5. Colin Morton, 'Industrial Village', *The Coracle*, No. 50, March 1967, p. 21.

CHAPTER EIGHT

The Three Faces of the Iona Community

'Action Now'. In the early days of the Iona Community this was one of George MacLeod's favourite aphorisms. What mattered was not what men said but what they did. There was plenty of talk in the Church but very little action. The Iona Community stood for action, whatever the action might be.

It was, therefore, inevitable that people should ask what the Iona Community was doing rather than what it was saying. They were hungry for action. They wanted to see what the Community was doing.

The difficulty in answering the question was that people were not only looking for different things but they were seeing different things. People differed in their interests and therefore in what they wanted to see. But the difficulty was greater. They were not just looking at the same thing in differing ways. They were looking at quite different things. For the Iona Community was a complex organisation with multiform activities. It showed at least three faces to the world and these three faces often seemed to be looking in quite different directions. In any case they could not all be seen at the same time.

In this complexity the Iona Community was different from the many post-war experiments with which it was compared and with all of which it felt a certain kinship. Most of the other enterprises worked on the principle of having one specific limited objective. There were industrial missions set up in

Britain and America to explore the way of Christian thought and action in industry. There were centres of adult education, such as the Evangelical Academies in Germany and the Laity Institutes in the Netherlands, engaged in the education of men and women for a new kind of life in Europe. Each of these tended to have its own particular emphasis — on the professions, or trade unions, or education or the arts. There were houses concerned with some form of evangelism or with spiritual up-building or with healing.

The Iona Community could never claim a like simplicity. It did not conform to any recognised type. It could not be defined simply as a retreat centre, or a lay institute, or a postgraduate college for training ministers, or an industrial mission or a centre for congregational renewal. It was all these things but all of them together. And it was something more: it was a community. If the enquirer's interest was exclusively on only one of these things he could get a very distorted and frustrating view of the Iona Community. People often come to Iona looking for one particular thing in the Community. Sometimes they find it. More often they find something quite different. The result is a diversity of conflicting and even contradictory reports of what the Iona Community is like and what it is doing. And none of them is complete. And so the tidy-minded find the Iona Community an odd, anomalous body, difficult to pigeon-hole, hard to assess for success or failure.

The reason is that it has never had one particular line of action or concern, even though at times it has talked as if it had. It has always been engaged in a multiplicity of activities. If its being a community gives it its peculiar character, it is perhaps this variety of activity that gives it its particular significance. It is not trying to test some particular theory or to prove the efficacy of some line of action. It is concerned with the general actions of people in many areas of life in Church and society. The effect of anything it does depends on how far other people respond and how far their life is affected. For life is never lived along one line only. It would seem that the historic movements of reformation or renewal in the Church, such as the rise of monasticism or the Reformation or the foreign missionary movement of last century, depended, not on a group of men making an experiment, but on social ferment among men generally, on a willingness to find new ways of living and, over it all and sustaining it all, a persistent but bewildered search for a new understanding of the Faith. These were all tied up together and often in apparent conflict. But until something happens along all these lines, nothing will happen of lasting significance.

This is not to suggest that this kind of ferment is working in the Iona Community except in so far as it is working among men generally. The Iona Community knows that a specialised experiment, however efficient, is never by itself effective. It knows in its own life that many lines have to meet if anything is to be achieved, even if everything appears to be in a tangle and its individual members to be pulling in different ways.

And, indeed, the Iona Community can be rightly described in three different and quite distinct ways. First, simply and graphically, the Iona Community as George MacLeod saw it at the beginning and continued to see it; second, the Iona Community as its members know it; and third, the Iona Community which others know and the world sees. And these are not merely different ways of describing the same thing. They are different things in themselves. They interact indeed and none is adequate in itself. Together they make up the Iona Community which is something that no-one can see easily or fully. But if the Iona Community achieves anything at all it is because it is this odd trinity, looking out on the world with three quite different faces.

In any attempt to assess the success or failure of the Iona Community during the first thirty years of its life it is advisable to think at first of these three aspects separately.

I

There is, then, first the Iona Community as George MacLeod saw it at the beginning — a practical scheme for the training of young ministers. And this is how he continued to see it. When the work of rebuilding on Iona was coming to an end and discussion was imperative about the full future use of the completed Abbey, he put forward a passionate and cogently argued plea for its use as a centre of theological education. He was convinced that there was need for an alternative to the academic training of the faculties of theology in the four older Scottish universities. The suggested education would be more practical and corporate in the training it offered to ordinands. He saw it as based on the experience of the Iona Community and based on Iona, though men would not spend all their time there. It was intended to bring students away from academic life and into the secular life of the world. The scheme did not prove practicable. But his strong advocacy of it at so late a date indicated how strongly his original conception of the Iona Community as existing for the specific purpose of training ministers still held.

There is no question that it was for this purpose that the Iona Community was originally founded. George MacLeod resigned his charge of the parish of Govan because he was convinced that the Church had to find new ways to fulfil its mission in industrial Scotland. He knew from his own experience that no progress could be made in this until some radical change was made in the training of the ministers of the Church. They had to learn to live and work with other men. They had to learn that it was action and not words that mattered. This was why he went to Iona and undertook the long job of completing the rebuilding of the ruined Abbey. Young ministers were to learn to live and work with other men in conditions that made it impossible to escape the questions and the tensions of a confined corporate life.

But it was not only George MacLeod who saw the Iona Community in this light. The young ministers who were the first members also saw it in the same light. This was the attraction of the new community. This was why they joined. They were interested in it because they thought that it could give them some of the training and experience which the colleges did not and perhaps could not offer and of which they felt a desperate need. They dreaded the loneliness which lay before them in the parish ministry. They liked the idea of belonging with others in a community. They knew that this was promised them but it was their professional concern that led them to join. And this still holds. Those who were later to join from outside Scotland — from America and elsewhere overseas and from England — were not so aware of the nature of the Community and of what its membership offered them. They were more intent on the practical training and experience that were available. And because the Iona Community is seen abroad in this light a Leader of the Community on visiting the United States finds that it is to the theological seminaries that he is primarily and constantly invited. The Iona Community is there regarded as having something specific to say about theological education and something practical to offer in the way of clerical experience.

The World Council of Churches seemed also to recognise this as the special sphere of the Community's interests. When it was preparing its report on theological education for its Assembly in Uppsala in July 1968, its secretary wrote asking for the Community's help. He did this specifically because, so far as he knew, the Iona Community was the only body with which the World Council was in touch which was concerned practically with the corporate training of young ministers *after* they had left theological college. This seemed almost unbelievable. But it must have been true for I was invited to the World Consultation on Theological Education which met in London in the summer of 1967 to prepare the final report.[1]

The Iona Community was founded on this insight of George MacLeod's and has always seen the task of training its minister members as a practical and primary obligation. It remains a basic task and the Community continues to give much thought to it. George MacLeod was undoubtedly right in seeing the reformation of the training of the clergy as urgent. In the present situation of the Church the clergy can prevent things from happening by doing nothing or assist things to happen by doing different things which they have not done in the past. At a time of change in the Church as in the State careful thought has to be given to the position and efficiency of its civil service. George MacLeod was also right in his conviction that theological education had to be brought into contact with ordinary life and in particular with the life of industrial men. He could be criticised for seeing the training of the clergy as all-important, the only problem. But resistance to the idea that the fundamental question is the education of the laity and not of the clergy has always been strong.

How effective has been this, the primary and still fundamental aspect of the work of the Iona Community? There can be no doubt that it met the need of many theological students. The numbers prove this. In the ten years from 1950 to 1959 young ministers joining were 5, 3, 6, 13, 9, 8, 10 and 10. This annual intake brought incalculable benefits to the Iona Community. These new ministers kept the Community young. They prevented the fate that overtakes many societies and institutions — of becoming a staid and ageing group of weary men. They made each year their contribution of question, protest and discovery. The price paid was that the Iona Community became increasingly clerical. This was inevitable when young ministers were the only men

1. Steven G. Mackie, *Patterns of Ministry: Theological Education in a Changing World* (Collins, 1969).

deliberately recruited and when the response was so good.

But what did the men themselves gain? It was not often what they would have liked to have got. Some of them were looking for a theology or a programme or some technique. And these they did not get. At least if they got them they had to find them for themselves. From working day by day by the side of the craftsmen they soon found that the ordinary man was not in the least interested in their theological arguments. If they wanted to talk to them they had to learn their language. They were living in close quarters not only with the craftsmen but with each other and with a motley group of visitors. The student's prerogative to a private life of his own was continually being challenged. And all the time they were taking part in daily worship with other people. In the fifties the ministers' group was becoming ecumenical. From other churches there came in those years 2, 3, 4, 4, 1, 3 and 2 — from a variety of denominations in the United States, Canada, Australia, New Zealand, England, Wales and Ireland. This mixing up of traditions and opinions was extremely valuable, especially for Scots students.

This intense period of corporate living on Iona was short, only three months. But it was the creative experience, partly because it was the initial experience and partly because it was here that men got to know their fellows. This short period on Iona was followed by twenty-one months of service in a selected parish under a senior member of the Community. The benefit of this longer period was much more variable and uncertain. It was largely outside the control of the Iona Community. But some benefits were clear. The young member had an older fellow-member with whom he could talk and — perhaps more important — he had at the monthly meetings of the Community the opportunity of discussing his problems with others in the same position and with those a little ahead. In most churches the position of a minister in a parish or congregation is a very lonely one and many cannot

113

stand the strain. Members of the Iona Community seem to be better able to do so, just because they don't feel so lonely. Many who have been through this initial training have after a while dropped out of full membership. This has been particularly true of those who have gone back to their own country and have rightly become engrossed in their own community there. But the number of those who have dropped out of the ministry has been small. Their training in the Iona Community seems to have meant a lot to them.

Justification for the Iona Community's original and continuing concern with education of the ministry could be found in the work done by its minister-members in their parishes, in specialised ministeries as industrial, hospital and university chaplains, as teachers in universities, colleges and schools and in ecumenical jobs of various kinds. But the main justification lies in the vital and inescapable importance of the issue. It is this commitment that ties the Iona Community into the ordinary life of the Church and prevents it from becoming merely theoretical.

II

But if the first recognisable face of the Community is still as George MacLeod saw it and still sees it, it is not the face that its members now recognise as theirs. They see this first face as describing the way men come into the Iona Community but not as revealing the Community as they know it. The Community they know is something quite different. For them the Iona Community is a free, open society of men who are not in training or under orders but are responsible for their own affairs while sharing a common idea of the demands of life and a loosely applied mutual discipline. This sense of family, based on friendship and a common view of life, is what the words 'The Iona Community' mean to its members. It is significant that when the members of the Community break into smaller, local groups they call those 'family groups'. It is also significant that increasingly the members regard these family groups, at which wives are present, as the basic structure of the life of the Community. When members of the Iona Community talk about the Community it is of this life of fellowship that they are thinking. It is a life known only to the full members of the Community. It is essentially exclusive. So it sometimes rouses resentment, or at least irritation, among those who are associated with the Community but who are not or cannot be full members. A society that is trying to find a more demanding and a more satisfying life for itself is bound to appear to others as a secret society. It is the more mystifying because it makes its demands on its associates, its friends and anyone who comes in touch with it.

There is no known type of religious society to which the Iona Community can be said to conform. There are plenty of private societies that reveal some of its characteristics. But the Iona Community is not just a private society. It does not exist just to live its own life. It sees itself as having a mission and undertakes work to promote it. In this it might be compared to a religious order. But there is a great difference, even from the Community of Taizé which also belongs to the Reformed Church. The members of the Iona Community have taken no vows. Their commitment is to find their life with other men in the common responsibilities of family, work and politics. So when we look round for some other similar organisation we are in difficulties. There are communities, such as Lea Abbey, whose members are bound together far more closely in work and economic discipline. They are a society of men and women who are living together and are all the time engaged in maintaining their estate and running their programme of conferences. It is as if the Iona Community were limited to those working on Iona. This is very different from a fellow-ship of some hundred and fifty members scattered all over the world and all doing their own jobs and seeing the place of their obedience in the common life of the world. The fact that there tends to be a clash between the close group on Iona and the wider life of the Community as a whole is an indication of the essential difference. But despite this concern with finding their own way of life and despite their involvement in the work of the world, the members of the Iona Community have property to maintain and conferences and camps to run and Community House in Glasgow to supervise and staff to appoint and accounts to pass. And this is probably a salutary necessity, even though by some members it is regarded as an imposed burden and an irritating distraction. They feel that their real concern is with their life together in the Community. They wish that they had more time to give to it. And they may well be right.

For what men and women want today is to know how to live responsibly and joyfully in the modern world: in their homes, in their jobs, in the common life of their neighbourhood, in the life of the nation and in the life of the world. The closed, religious community is of little help to them, except as an escape. The community that is essentially a staff united in a common and self-directed job does not easily interpret life to those who are working in all kinds of jobs, with all sorts of people and under various forms of direction and control. Most people cannot get out of this situation of temporary commitment and limited responsibility. They want to find how to live more purposeful and more enjoyable lives where they are, with their families and neighbours, in their leisure and in their work, with their problems and their hopes. A community sharing the same conditions but with opportunities for choice because they have learned to share their common life, should be able to offer some kind of support. But how? How does it do this without becoming self-conscious as an example, always talking about itself and so losing its health? How does it support its own members, to say nothing of other people? How does it prevent itself from becoming a society of like-minded people, supporting all sorts of good causes?

Can the members of the Iona Community, in their life together, claim to have achieved anything for themselves and for others? This is an impossible question to answer adequately. Any life together — in family, group, party or church — achieves something. Through our life together we learn whatever we do learn from life, of good and bad. Perhaps the question had better be put differently: has the deliberately chosen form of corporate life of the Iona Community contributed something that otherwise would have been missed? The members of the Iona Community would certainly claim that it has. It has fostered a reliance on each other that has supported them in their decisions and actions. It has also broken down the bastions of privacy and widened the area of mutual discussion. In particular, money, work and politics have been the topics of conversation and debate. This has often led to more decisive actions that might otherwise have been expected. Discipline has not been interpreted solely in terms of prayer and worship but in terms of use of time and the use of money. It can well be claimed that this has had its effect on groups outside the Iona Community and in the life of the Church as a whole.

So, for all the difficulty of finding how it helps other people, this face of the Iona Community may well be the most significant in the end. For it deals with the sphere of ordinary living and this is what in the end alone matters. It may be that it is only as we give ourselves wholeheartedly and without forethought to our business of living that we can make any contribution at all to new life in the world.

III

But the Iona Community has another face and perhaps it is the most significant. It is the face that looks out on the world — the Iona Community as others see it and as they want to see it.

They are not particularly interested in the Community as George MacLeod sees it. They do not feel any special concern for the training of the clergy. They may be curious about the life that the full members of the Community have among themselves. But they know that it is not for them. They feel that the Iona Community — or at least Iona — has something for them and that they are entitled to get it. They form the great majority of those who make such a claim. They represent the overriding reason for the very existence of the Iona Community. Therefore it will not be surprising that this third face with which the Iona Community looks out on the world should demand the most attention.

This is inevitable. To think of others is to get back to the origins of the Iona Community. It was the plight of the unemployed on Clydeside during the great economic depression of the thirties that brought the Community into being. The form of the Community was determined by the needs of men — the isolation of the industrial worker on one hand and the isolation of the Church on the other. The prayer of the Iona Community from the beginning and used every day since is that 'hidden things may be revealed to them and new ways found to touch the hearts of men'. Ministers were trained for the more effective service of others. The Abbey was restored that it might be fully used by others. The new enterprises that were open to the Community after the war made wider and more explicit this concern for others: through Community House in Glasgow, through camps and other forms of youth work, in industry and politics. Concern was thus extended from those in need — the unemployed and youth — to those in power — those in industry, in trade unions and in management, and those in politics, including all church people.

Money flowed in to the Community in generous gifts, large and small. George MacLeod spent a great deal of time, energy and imagination in the raising of money. But this money was to finance this work for others. The Abbey, for the completion of the restoration of which the Community paid, does not belong to the Community. It is open for the use of all and the courses, conferences and retreats that the Community arranges are for all who want to come. Community House and the youth camps are not run for the benefit of members of the Community. The staff are mainly engaged in the promotion of this work for others. The Iona Community is indeed very scrupulous in seeing that their own expenses in travel and meetings come out of the personal contribution of members. This whole financial emphasis is an indication of the essential purpose of the Iona Community as being for others.

These others are of many kinds. But they all have one thing in common. They come in a personal, almost a private, capacity. Theirs is not a professional interest like that of the ministers or the craftsmen or others who join as full members. Their interest has been aroused by what they have seen or by what they have heard. They make their own contact and find something that speaks to their condition. Almost certainly at the beginning and still, two things about the Iona Community made an instant appeal. One thing was the emphasis on action. The other was that it was visible. This was the great gift of Iona. Action seen in the simple setting of Iona aroused a curiosity that was immediate and an interest that was often lasting. In a broadcast talk in those early days Nathaniel Micklem explained the appeal thus:

'This Iona Movement is all of a piece: the rebuilding of the old ruins, the coupling of intellectual work with manual, the bringing of the common loaves to Church, the fishing-nets round the Holy Table (at another centre), the direct prayer, the insistence that politics and craftsmanship and economics and drama and home religion are not to be separated, the holy indignation that the Church has become to some considerable extent a coterie out of touch with life.'

The signs today would be put differently. But it is still this same simple visible unity that makes many people feel that they have a claim to call Iona theirs and even to claim that they belong in some unofficial way to the Iona Community itself.

What they found on Iona was not the sight of other people doing things but something into which they could enter and make their own. They found worship which was their worship and discussion in which they could participate. They met other people and did things with them and learned about their opinions, achievements and problems. Whether they were young people in camp or older people in conference at the Abbey, they might well confess that they had got a new vision of the world and a new way of life opening for them and new things to do when they got home or old things to do in a new way.

It is right to see the effect of Iona in these few simple things. The contact that men and women made was probably for a week, or at most for two weeks, as a camper or a member of a conference or more probably as a casual holiday-maker on the island. But it was the visible and corporate simplicity of the contact that was influential. It brought the chance to do a little thinking and a little talking with others about life and their jobs and their faith. It raised the challenge to further action in industry or in politics or in the life of the Church. There is no question that it was Iona in particular that sparked all this off. But it was never confined to the island. Iona was for all a place that they left to go home, back to the demands and questions of daily life. And the Iona Community was there if they wanted to use it for they took it with them.

For they could make their own commitment to life as they returned home. They could keep in touch with Iona and with others of a like mind through becoming Associates of the Iona Community, sharing in the discipline and being kept informed of what was going on. The Association expressed the desire of many to keep in personal touch with Iona and the Iona

Community. It also expressed their determination to take back into their lives at home something of the vision of unity that they had seen on Iona. It was for this that they held regular meetings, conferences and retreats in the cities of Scotland and England.

In its efforts to touch as large a number of other people as possible the Iona Community did not, of course, confine itself to Iona or to the Associates. Without Iona it is doubtful whether any wide impact on others would have been made. The Associates have a vital importance in the life of the Community because they are the constant bridge between the Community and the world of other people. In a sense Iona was a natural symbol which was there for the using. Other deliberate means of attraction, discussion and commitment had to be devised to widen the range of contact and to bring Iona down to the industrial and political earth, such as Community House, the youth camps, industrial and political activities. These were all for the benefit and use of others, not of the members of the Community. Through these means many came into contact with the Iona Community, found that it had something relevant to offer them and that they could in some sort of way claim the Community as theirs.

This was the face of the Iona Community that looked out on the world. And this was the face that brought the world to Iona. It was this concern for other people — and George MacLeod's travels — that forged the Community's links with the outside world. Neither clerical training nor mission — industrial or evangelistic — nor spiritual formation could tie the Iona Community in to the postwar world. What was common to progressive movements in that world was the desire to find the way of awakening ordinary people to their political, social and industrial responsibilities and of giving them some training for action. It was on this side of its life and work that the Iona Community made contact with the outside world. More particularly it was through this work that it formed constitutional links with kindred movements in other countries and with the Ecumenical Movement.

These links were forged many years ago. Soon after the end of the war, in 1947, I was invited to attend a small conference convened by the provisional World Council of Churches at the Ecumenical Centre recently opened at Bossey in Switzerland. It was attended by people concerned about or engaged in the business of the education of the laity in postwar Europe. It was a small but significant group. There was Reinold von Thadden-Trieglaff, discussing the need of developing in Germany something of the democratic life he had known in Britain and already planning the Kirchentag which was to grow into the vast exercise in political education which we now know. There was Eberhard Muller in agony over the collapse of Germany and the spiritual, political and economic problems that faced men there, but already creating the Evangelical Academy at Bad Boll. There was A. W. Kist, then of Kerk and Wereld in the Netherlands, aware of how the Church there before the war had not been truly in the world and had to learn to get there. There were others from Sweden, Hungary and Greece: and to help with the study Professor Eichrodt of Basel, Jean Bosc of Paris, Wolfgang Schweitzer and Paul Tournier of Geneva, and J. C. Hoekendijk, then already the theologian of mission. The purpose of the consultation was thus expressed in the words of the original minute:

> 'L'Institut Oecumenique de Bossey a convoqué du 10 au 14 avril 1947 un groupe d'hommes specialisés dans le travail accompli dans le cadre de l'Eglise pour atteindre les laics dans leurs diverses professions. It s'agissait de provoquer un échange de vues et de jeter les bases d'une collaboration plus effective entres les organisations pursuivant un but similaire.'

We reported on the things we were trying to do. We were painfully aware of the international tensions created by war and of the very different social and political conditions prevailing in each country. But we were equally aware of the common nature of our tasks and of their immense difficulty. The conference decided that some kind of organisation was needed as a centre of study and information on the subject of the education of the laity. It also decided that a conference be held to discuss industry in the following year.

Iona lies very far away on the outer fringe of Europe. The Iona Community was pretty insular. Indeed in the forties every country was very much concerned with its own affairs; and so was every centre. And perhaps at the time the Iona Community tended to look westward to America rather than eastward to Europe. But other things were happening to forge closer links with Europe. Because of George MacLeod's writing and speaking and his ability to appeal to the imagination of men and because the Iona Community had existed before the war and was regarded as a pioneer in new ways, Europe began coming to Iona. Students came — from France, from Switzerland, from Germany. Leaders from the centres in Europe came — from Sigtuna in Sweden, from Taizé in France, from Bad Boll and Arnoldsheim in Germany. They came to see what Iona was doing; and to tell us what they were doing which was far more valuable for us. The contacts were, indeed, not only one way. In the early fifties Tom Colvin, the Youth Secretary of the time, frequently visited the Continent and brought the youth associates into contact with youth in Europe, especially in Eastern Europe.

Other actions followed from the conference at Bossey. I was asked by the World Council of Churches to gather together a group to study and prepare a report on Evangelism in Scotland, as one of a series of Ecumenical Studies. This was published in 1954.

In 1953 I had the opportunity of spending June in Germany. My main engagement was in Berlin, still sadly in ruins, assisting in conferences organised by the Ecumenical Institute at Bossey for people from East Germany. I also visited several

I.C.—5

Evangelical Academies and the Gossner Mission at Mainz-Kastel, which, of all the centres I saw in Germany, was nearest to Iona, in its manual work, its training of young ministers and its contact with industrial men.

In 1956 the Department of the Laity of the World Council of Churches brought out a booklet entitled *Signs of Renewal*. It was edited by Hans-Ruedi Weber and bore as its sub-title 'The Life of the Lay Institutes of Europe'. With the same desperate hopefulness that inspired the title, Kathleen Bliss in the introduction explained the aim of the new movements:

> 'One task of these new institutions is the direct service of the Church and of the many lay movements by stimulating and expertly instructing the laity to perform their own inalienable duty as the people of God in the world of daily life. But there is a second task, that of an open and disinterested service of society in its present needs and its God-appointed tasks. . . . The new Christian institutions described in this book have this matter of the Church's outreach towards government and industry, education and the arts much in mind, and some are directed wholly towards effecting contact between the Church and some sphere of ordinary life with which it is conspicuously out of touch.'[2]

The Iona Community was included among these signs of renewal along with the Evangelical Academies of Germany, the Lay Institutes of the Netherlands and Switzerland, Sigtuna in Sweden, Agapé in Italy, Glay in France and a few others. This was how the Iona Community was seen by those in Europe and beyond and by the world Church. This was how it was seen as relevant to the postwar world. It was a sign of renewal because it was committed to the education of the laity. It was the face that it turned to the secular world that attracted the attention of men.

But more was needed than mention in a book. The bringing

2. Hans-Ruedi Weber (ed.), *Signs of Renewal* (World Council of Churches, 1st edition, 1956), p. 56.

of the Iona Community — and other British centres — into lively and constitutional contact with kindred centres in Europe was due in great measure to Mark Gibbs, the English Secretary of the now fully established Association of Directors of European Lay Centres (now called the Ecumenical Association of Directors of Academies and Laity Centres in Europe) and an Associate of the Iona Community. He felt that the British centres had to get into Europe and that they had something significant to contribute, especially in the sphere of political responsibility.

As a result the annual conference of the Association was held on Iona in 1964. During a week of endless sunshine we introduced the directors of the European centres to the rigours of a stormy climate and of a 'dry' island, to the demands of daily worship and of politics, especially in the area of war and peace. The union of worship and politics disconcerted most of those who came. Some welcomed worship but without politics. Others were happy with politics but without worship. Since then the Iona Community has tried to play a full part in Europe and in wider ecumenical contacts. But when domestic difficulties are pressing, this interest unfortunately goes.

There can be no doubt that we gain a great deal from knowing more of the way those in other countries face our common problems. There is even less doubt that we in Scotland have more need than anyone else to learn from other countries. At the same time there is no doubt that the British centres had their contribution to make in the European Association, and specifically on the importance of politics and theology and on their inter-relation. The Iona Community was unique among all these centres in being a community with a continuing membership and not just an institution with a staff which sometimes changed. This continuity of a community meant that in its life and thinking it has always been tied down to earth by the involvement of its members in their jobs in church, industry and society. However much tempted at times to do so the Iona Community could never pursue one particular line to the disregard of others, as was the avowed purpose of many of the other centres. It therefore appeared to them to dissipate its energies and to move very slowly. But it could never escape for long into a particular interest away from the general interests of the mass of people. And these general interests, stated crudely, are religion and politics — how we see human destiny and how we organise our life.

This contribution of the Iona Community to the ecumenical movement in the area of laity education was not probably very significant, for it had little obvious effect. It is important because it illustrated the most important aspect of the Community's work. This was what the Iona Community had been founded to do. This was the mainspring of all its activities. If the Community fails in this third aspect of its work, in its contact with people in their ordinary lives, in their work and in their politics, nothing else that it does will matter very much.

Can we make any claim for the Iona Community along this third line? it is a difficult question to answer: much more difficult than to answer the same question about the other two aspects. When we considered the first face of the Iona Community — the training of ministers — we could count them and name them and know their opinions. When we considered the Iona Community in the life of its members we were dealing with something less tangible but something definite in its limits. When we consider the efforts of the Iona Community 'to touch the hearts of men' and to affect their public lives it is difficult to say anything and presumptuous to make claims. It is difficult because we are not dealing with other people but with ourselves and our actions in the world. For we are involved with all other men. We are involved in their actions and they in ours. Perhaps we can describe with confidence how we educate ourselves for responsible action in the world. We cannot with presumption assess the unknown actions of numberless other people. And yet the Iona Community can find no justification for its years of existence except in the actions of countless men and women in the world today.

We can't measure these. But there are certain things that we can say.

Most of the criticism of and opposition to the Iona Community from its beginning was on account of its political teaching and actions. This was at least an indication that its teachings and actions were noticed and that it in this negative way affected the discussion and thinking of some people. But there were more positive effects. Many people, through Iona and Community House in Glasgow, were awakened to the importance of political questions and some were moved to participate actively in political life. The Associates give sure evidence of this in their conferences and correspondence. And the Associates in their hundreds are fairly representative of the others in their thousands who would confess to the Community's influence even though its members knew nothing about what they are now doing.

The conferences, classes, courses and seminars held through the years on Iona and in Community House may at times have seemed unproductive of results. But there is no doubt that they stimulated thought and aroused some to political and social actions they would not otherwise have thought of taking. Some were set on a new direction in their life-work. The fact that the programme went on year after year on Iona meant that people could come back on occasion or regularly, could find renewal and refreshment, could bring new points for discussion and could challenge the Community's routine and conventions. And such people were not limited to those who enrolled for conferences. They included people on holiday on the island and even day tourists. When we take laity education seriously we have to remember its basic informality.

Community House as a place of meeting in the centre of Glasgow brought people together for the study and discussion of the problems of a changing city. Groups could meet together there who could not otherwise meet. Many active organisations which now go their own way came into existence in Community House and because of the action of its leaders. The Glasgow Marriage Guidance Council and the Scottish Committee for War on Want were two early examples. And there are many later ones. These are only an indication of the Iona Community's work in widening the area of people's social and political concern and of setting them on the way to action. This widening of the area of concern and stimulus to action was probably the Community's main contribution to the life of the Church of Scotland, particularly in the fields of political action and industrial responsibility.

It is obvious that the Iona Community can make no proper claims or take credit for what others have done. If it had any effect it was because others responded and acted on their own. We are confident that they did.

These three lines of the Iona Community's life — the training of ministers, the life together of the members, and its work for others — may seem quite distinct. They certainly operate in different areas and with different sets of people. But they are all intrinsically parts of the one enterprise, and all necessary parts. And perhaps this triple nature of its life and work explains the odd uniqueness of the Iona Community. It may be that here lies whatever of value it has to offer to men and women today. Any attempt to find new ways of life and service for Christians in the world today will remain something on which to write a report unless somehow it brings people in ever widening circles into personal commitment in their daily lives and into an honest endeavour to understand the relevance of the faith for today and at the same time is concerned with the actual structures of the society it seeks to serve. No member of the Iona Community would claim that it has achieved this. But the experience of the Community does demonstrate the value of continuity and the need of some kind of corporate commitment at the level of ordinary life.

This triple nature of the work of the Iona Community naturally raises many problems in administration. It is not always easy to maintain a proper balance. It is easy for one line to get all the attention at one particular time, of crisis or of opportunity. The staff, and particularly the senior staff, will often find themselves in a difficult position, for their relation to each aspect of the work is different.

When we look at the first face of the Iona Community and think of its original intention to give a new kind of corporate experience to young ministers, we remember the annually changing fellowship of young men on Iona for the summer as they prepare for their work in their parishes. The relationship of the resident staff to this group is clear. They are in the position of college tutors. And as the men are newly out of college and are expecting further teaching, they expect and accept this relationship. It is a relationship of youth and age, of conflict and of understanding. The staff is expected to advise, to stimulate thought, to be the target of questions, objections and rebellion to those who still think and behave as students. Each year has its own peculiar pattern of men but with all of them at that most interesting moment of transition from study to a job. It may be an awkward experience for the men. It is a stimulating experience for the staff. The relationship is enjoyable perhaps because it is simple.

When we think of the second face of the Iona Community as a free fellowship of responsible men, we see the position of the staff in a very different light. The Leader or any other member of staff is basically in no different a position from any other member. They are a band of equals. He has no power to direct them. He is under the same discipline as they are. The Leader is, indeed, the chairman of the Community and has the authority that this position gives him. From his position and wider contact with other members he is in a position to give advice and help. But members are free to take it or not as they see fit. The advice and help of other members is as likely to be asked. This is not an easy position for members of staff who are at the same time members of the Community, employed by the Community and the spokesmen of the Community in the eyes of others.

On this two points should be made. One is a small one. In recent years the Iona Community has appointed to its junior staff men and women who are not members of Community. This can increase the sense of division between membership of the Iona Community and the work that is done in its name. The other point is more important. The use of the title 'Leader' is unfortunate, though it is difficult to find a better. As a description of the relationship of a senior member of staff to his fellow members of Community it is both misleading and dangerous. His position poses the problem of authority in an open, democratic society. It is a problem for a small society like the Iona Community. It is as urgent a problem for our great society. It confronts us in the organisation of industry, in the Church and in national affairs. It may be that one of the most useful things that the Iona Community could do would be to find out something about this from their own experience.

The third face of the Iona Community is turned to the world. The position of the staff is here again quite different. As, apart from the Associates, there is no means of organisation of those others whom the Iona Community seeks to serve, the staff is here in much more of a position of authority and power. If the staff does not organise a programme of conferences and discussion at Iona, in Community House in Glasgow and in the youth camps, nothing is likely to happen. This is one of the problems of adult education. It has to be informal. There can be no compulsion on people to participate. It depends on a free response of interest. And yet it cannot easily be self-directed. The directing of a non-directive programme is a difficult task, for which few people are trained, least of all those who have had a theological education. It has not been the task for which members of staff have been selected by the Iona Community. Yet it could be argued that it has been their most important work. It entails keeping contact with people, being responsive to their questions and needs and being open to try new ways. Our biggest opportunities were here: and our biggest failure.

This wide difference in the types of work involved and in the varying relationships with different types of people is probably the reason why the Iona Community finds the business of finding, appointing and directing staff very difficult.

It has been given prominence here because this record of personal impressions of the Iona Community has been written from the point of view of a member of its staff. The report of the majority of members whose life-work has not been in the employment of the Community but in ecclesiastical or secular jobs outside would be different. The staff-member may be very prejudiced but at least he sees most of the game.

But in the end it is the Community that alone matters. This is not merely because it appoints the staff and is the final arbiter of policy. It is rather because the Community has the strength of continuity. And continuity means the possibility of new life and openness to the future. Nothing is ever proved: nothing is ever finished.

CHAPTER NINE

The Future of the Iona Community

On New Year's Day, 1967, George MacLeod announced to the Press that he intended to resign from the leadership of the Iona Community. This was the first intimation given to any member of the Community. The occasion was the announcement on the same day in the New Year Honours List of his elevation to a life peerage. His way of announcing his decision was a shock to the members of the Iona Community.

I had been Deputy Leader for many years. I was convinced that my appointment as Deputy must come to an end with his retiral as Leader. I was also anxious to leave the situation as wide open as possible for the members of the Community to plan for the future. I therefore intimated my resignation.

As this account of the early years of the Iona Community has been a very personal one and from the point of view of one who served on the staff of the Community, it comes to an end in 1967. The Iona Community has not, of course, come to an end. Nor has my membership of the Community come to an end. It has, indeed, proved of great interest and happiness to be an ordinary member. But to continue a personal account from so changed a point of view would have been difficult of achievement, distracting to the reader and perhaps unfair to others. A continuing, similar account of the second stage of the history of the Iona Community should be written by someone as involved since 1967 as I was before.

In that account there will be much to tell. And it will be a different story. The Iona Community has had to make difficult adjustments. It has had to adjust to the end of dependence on a charismatic leader. It has had to get used to the idea of no more rebuilding having to be done on Iona. It has had to waken up to a rapidly changing situation in the world. Ian Reid, who was appointed Leader in the summer of 1967, had the awkward task of guiding the Community through this difficult period. He has fulfilled it with dedication, determination and grace. The Abbey on Iona has in these years seen a great development in its programme, both in the length of the season and in the nature of its activities. Community House in Glasgow has changed its policy to meet the new social problems of the changing city. But perhaps the biggest change has been in the membership of the Community itself, not only because of the annual addition of new young members, including more articulate laymen and the dropping out of some of the older men, but also from a greater freedom in its way of life. And now in the middle seventies it faces the third stage of its history, with the appointment of a new Leader, the third in succession.

To forecast the future may be fashionable but it is foolish. It certainly would be rash to attempt to say how the Iona Community will go forward. It would be dangerous to say how it ought to go. It might be more pertinent to discuss whether the Community should have a future at all: whether it has not fulfilled its task, proved what it set out to prove and plotted paths which others must now follow. When in early days George MacLeod and others both within and outside the Community talked of it as an experiment, this temporary nature of the Iona Community was a constant theme. It was never envisaged as continuing indefinitely. It was recognised that it might outlive its usefulness: that to disband might be a sign of success, to continue the symbol of failure. This question might well be discussed but I leave the discussion to the members of the Iona Community in the third stage of its history.

The fact that they are there ready to discuss the question indicates that the Iona Community has at least an immediate future open to it. It is no longer an experiment but a community with a life of its own. It is like a family. So long as a family is made up of living people and they are bound together by a common way of life and have a place to live in or to come back to, it continues as a visible, effective social unit. Without these assets it disappears. And families do disappear.

What are the assets that ensure that the Iona Community will continue for — to use a modern, awkward and contradictory phrase — the 'foreseeable future'? For its present assets will determine the kind of life it will live in the years ahead. The Iona Community is no more likely than a family to be free to indulge in revolutionary changes in its way of life. It can only use its assets. It can use or misuse them in a variety of ways. It may develop them. It may dissipate them. It cannot completely get away from them.

The assets of the Iona Community can be listed under three headings similar to those of the family — the continuity of the membership, the experience that underlies their attitudes and their way of doing things, and a place that is their own. These inalienable assets determine how the Iona Community will face the future.

Continuity is the proof and condition of any society. A social group is composed of people and it continues to exist so long as they remain in it. In the discontinuity that oppresses many people in their lives today anything that offers the comfort and stability of continuity is welcomed. It is the great attraction of the Church for many. It is the reason for the existence of many societies. We have seen how the continuity expressed in the membership differentiates the Iona Community from many of its kindred institutions of the present time. The fact that it is not just a staff doing a particular job, as in an industrial mission, but a society of members all in jobs of their own slows down its action on any particular line and prevents any rapid change of policy. But it is this continuity that ensures its future. And its continuity is of a unique kind, as is that of any society. It is a rope that ties it to its known past and leads it into an unknown future. It is a rope of many strands, made up of threads of many colours, which fade out and reappear, with some strong ones that seem constant. It's of an ever changing pattern because of the annual intake of new members and the changing circumstances in work and family of others, bringing a different strength and a new tension and varying colours each year. But all the new threads are spliced on an old rope that ties it in to the origins of the Community in Govan in 1938. We might say that George MacLeod is that original and permanent strand. But there are other lesser threads that tie it in the same way. Certainly the Iona Community cannot loosen itself from the rope that ties it to its origin without losing its sense of purpose. But there are hundreds of other threads giving strength to the rope and tying the Community into life at many points, in parish and factory, in office and college, in city and island, in Africa and India and America — the whole continuing but ever-altering succession of those who have belonged to the Iona Community and still do. And the continuity is made up not only of the seven score who are the full members at the present time, but of a much wider number, of those who have been members of the Community, of those who have served the Community, of those who have given help or derived help — all who feel in some quite personal way that they belong to Iona. The certainty of a future for the Iona Community is based on the present fact of so many people bound to each other in the present and tied to their past, as in a family, and so unable to escape their future.

The Iona Community can either develop this asset or dissipate it. It cannot leave it as it is, expecting it to remain unchanging. The members may be tempted to think that their community is large enough as it is and that they should take time to clarify and consolidate their present position, by adding no new members. This would be dangerous for without new life continuously injected it would sink into a torpor of discussion and inactivity. On the other hand it can develop its membership and accept the challenge of new life. This would almost certainly mean the recruitment of chosen categories of new members and the swinging of the balance from clerical to lay and a greater concern with political than with ecclesiastical life. There is no doubt that this second line is more likely to be followed than the first. The Iona Community is composed of people and will choose life rather than death. The question will be whether the change will be radical or simply token.

The second asset that the Iona Community possesses is its experience. When we talk about the experience of a group — of a family or a society or a Church or even a nation — we are thinking of the things that its members take for granted, that form the bases of their judgments and decisions, the things that at times they may try to understand better but never fundamentally question and rarely even discuss. These are the things we can know only corporately, not individually: in our life together, not in our solitude. These mysteries of our common life are perhaps of the same kind as the secrets of the kingdom which Jesus said his disciples possessed without their knowing it. These things of our corporate knowledge are almost impossible to state in words, for words are spoken individually. We express them more easily in song and dance, in art and music, in action and in worship and, unfortunately, also in violence. We are afraid of corporate knowledge but cannot live without it. This is one of the reasons why worship was from the beginning so basic to the life of the Community and still is. It is also the reason why some others suspect worship as an insidious form of persuasion.

It is, therefore, very difficult to put this experience into words. Any attempt to do so will inevitably be a prejudiced, individual interpretation of a corporate experience and, therefore, far from reliable. But there are certain things that the Iona Community knows in its bones and even though many of its members would describe them differently.

First, there is the experience of the corporate life that its members have all shared on Iona. It was to share a life of stark simplicity that George MacLeod brought the first members of the Community to Iona in 1938. The austerity has been softened in the passage of the years. But its simplicity remains. Participation in it is still the initiation of full members into the Community. It is easy to dismiss it as superficial and a bit of play-acting. The tensions that arise are proof that it is not. The abiding sensation is of the elemental conditions of life — the simplicity of wind and sun, of sea and mountain, dependence on weather and tide for essential supplies, reliance on others and there being no escape from them. This is what Iona means to members and what brings them constantly back. It is the sense that something of the very essence of life has been given to them: not mystical or romantic and certainly not sentimental but rather a very practical sense of the simple and beautiful reality of life. This is not to be adequately expressed in words and cannot be, but it is there, one of the things that members take for granted, the basis of the things they know together.

And because they have shared this simple life they have come to know each other in a new way — at least those who have shared the summer with them. They know that they belong to each other now. Of course we all know this mutual commitment in other spheres of life. It is one of the secrets of the joy of life. In those spheres we generally choose those to whom we'll be committed. The uniqueness of Iona is that they are given to us unsought and unknown. Even if later members drift apart or if something comes between them, as it can do, they are still aware of a bond that continues to unite them and which allows demands to be made. It is not an exclusive experience. It is an experience that lightens the whole of life and affects one's attitude to other people.

This experience has, I think, resulted in a certain suspicion of words, a dread of a too simple statement of purpose or belief even in those who advocate a more positive line. So we find a holding on to openness even at the cost of consistency. No one had been denied membership on account of his opinions. Refusal of membership has been confined to those who are not in a position to share the initial simple sharing of life on Iona. There have been times when some, including the founder, have been irritated by this openness and have tried to overcome it by imposing a stricter line. Even though anxious to see its members following more positive lines of action, the Iona Community has learned to resist the appeal of logic or the fear of seeming timidity. It knows that there is something more important than logic or consistency. It would find it hard to put a name to it. It seems to be a unity of mutual commitment and openness.

This openness is probably due to the fact that members of the Iona Community have always lived their lives in the world in jobs with other men. The Community has never been their whole life nor even the main part of their life, certainly not the world of their work, except for the staff. They know that what they do in the world matters far more than what they do in the Community. It is hence never enough to formulate a plan that can be operated only by a specially selected and trained group of their own members. What matters is what can be done in ordinary circumstances with the people who are there without special training and with limited resources. In the end it is only what works there that will be effective for long.

But with this feeling of where the reality of the world is to be found, there is also the conviction that there is no use talking without action. The Community has always known that there is no use calling on others to do things unless its members were doing something themselves. This might be some action for which the Community took responsibility, as in their camps for Borstal boys or their initial work in industry. But action would more probably be taken by members acting on their own in their differing situations and according to their own judgment. The Iona Community has been chary of having a political or theological line of its own. But it expects its members each to have his or her own line and to follow it.

These convictions and attitudes might be called the secrets of the Iona Community: the things the members know without stating them, difficult to express, impossible to define, fluid, constantly reacting to the contribution of new members and the understanding of new situations, but remaining fairly permanent and giving an indication how the Iona Community would be likely to think and act in the future. Critics of the Community — and they exist inside it as well as outside — demand something much more definite about principles and policy. They want something more categorically stated; something to attack or to expound. But the spring of our decisions and actions as individuals is generally very simple, far simpler than the reasons we give in justification. It is the same with groups. I am sure that this is so for the Iona Community.

But if continuity is variable and experience hard to define, Iona as the third asset of the Iona Community is certainly visible and inalienable. The Iona Community is fortunate in having a local habitation and a name. It can never dissociate itself from Iona. It is tied to Iona by its history. It is tied as securely by the interest and intentions of other people. It does not own Iona or the Abbey as it owns Community House in Glasgow. But Iona owns the Iona Community as Community House can never do. This is not just because Community House is liable to change, both through urban development and through the recognition of greatly changing needs. It is rather that the Community cannot escape from Iona, even if it wanted to. It is there. It is there for them through the experience of all its members in their formative, initial training. It is there for other people. It is their's with other people. The Community is possessed by Iona: as a reminder of the past — the far distant past and its immediate past, as a challenge for the future — as a job to be tackled, a problem to be solved, a life to be lived.

At times some members of the Community are tempted to regard Iona as a liability. They think that the Iona Community would be free to do all manner of new things if it were not saddled with an Abbey. They feel the burden of the tradition of the Abbey — their own tradition as much as a much older one. The feel the burden of responsibility for fitting in their activities to the needs of the programme on Iona. And an Abbey, by its type of building and by its associations, does, indeed, impose certain limitations on life and worship. But Iona is more than the Abbey. And it is Iona that is the inalienable asset for the Community — not to possess it but to be possessed by it, with the Abbey as a unique tool.

Iona holds the Community by the bonds of memory, association and affection. By these the Community is tied to Iona by its own past. But from its beginning Iona has spoken more strongly to the Community of the future than of the past. In 1939 a friend wrote a prayer and gave it to the Community. The Iona Community adopted it as its own prayer and has used it since constantly and regularly. It has as its final petition the words 'grant that a place of Thine abiding be established once again to be a sanctuary and a light'. In recent years a change has been made in these words. The prayer now reads 'that a place of Thine abiding be *continued* still to be a sanctuary and a light'. This change binds the Community even more strongly to Iona and the future.

'To be a sanctuary and a light' — but a sanctuary can be a place of escape and a light can be discreetly shaded. If the Iona Community were to give up its occupancy of the Abbey on

140

Iona the rush of those who would want to use it is easy to imagine: retreats of conventional or extravagant piety, happy holidays for those wanting a change. These would all be reflections of the desire of many people to find some kind of spiritual sanctuary and to see light of some sort in their lives. The only justification for the Community's continued use of the Abbey is that it meets this need in a wider context and a different way.

If the Iona Community does manage to do anything along this line it is faced with an almost intractable problem of its own use of Iona and because it cannot keep other people out of it. Any house demands upkeep and involves contact with neighbours. A mediaeval ruin that is restored makes more urgent demands. The Community cannot escape from the problem of what to do with it. It involves money and staff, programme and endless distractions. It forces the members of the Community to face the problem of their life together, on Iona and on the mainland. There can be an almost irresistible temptation to claim that they should be left alone to solve their own problem in peace. But this cannot be. Other people will not let them. They come to Iona. They claim Iona. They expect to find something for themselves on Iona. And it was for them that the Abbey was restored, the Community founded. The members of the Iona Community may at times feel that they have been saddled by the past with a building. But, in fact, the necessity of using the building and the inescapable meeting with other people of all sorts and of all opinions provide the Iona Community with the assurance of a future.

The problem of the use of Iona brings together men's suspicion of accepted religious ways and their fascination with them, the urgent desire of many to find a more satisfying and demanding pattern of personal living and the conviction that such a way must deal in a new way with the uncomfortably modern but ageless questions of sex and race and money. The

141

members of the Iona Community cannot escape this problem for it is inherent in their life together. But they cannot make Iona their private sanctuary because others come there with their wider experiences, more difficult questions and perhaps wilder hopes. If Iona is to continue to give light to men and women, the Community will need to encourage more and more people to come and make sure that they are as widely representative as possible. In the Christmas story the shepherds, the wise men and the devout came to see a light. In modern parlance their equivalents are the workers in industry, the scientists and politicians and the artists and rebels and all who are looking for something. It is the conjunction of the uncomfortable self-questioning of a small community and the anxieties and hopes, the seeking and the finding of innumerable other people that may ensure that Iona continues to be a sanctuary and a light.

But this is probably to verge on prophecy. It is certainly to indulge in wishful thinking. What is beyond doubt is that the Iona Community has assets, in its membership, its experience and in Iona, which promise it a future and afford it the chance to do something new, to do something still.